E I G G

Frontispiece: Garmisdale, an original line drawing by Caroline Gould.

EIGG

The Story of One Family's Love Affair with an Island

Peta Orr

Pentland Books
Edinburgh – Cambridge – Durham – USA

© Peta Orr, 2001

First published in 2001 by
Pentland Books
1 Hutton Close
South Church
Bishop Auckland
Durham

Email: manuscripts@pentlandpress.co.uk
Web: pentlandpress.co.uk

ISBN 1-85821-904-3

Typeset in Sabon
by Carnegie Publishing,
Carnegie House,
Chatsworth Road,
Lancaster

www.carnegiepub.co.uk

Printed and bound by
Antony Rowe Ltd,
Chippenham

CONTENTS

In memory of
Bill Orr
A Scot who loved Eigg and its people

Acknowledgements

I WOULD LIKE TO THANK the following people for all their help
with this book. My friends from Eigg, especially John Chester, the
Kirk family, Leslie Gowans and Angus MacKinnon. Jill Aldersley
for her lovely watercolour for the front cover and Caroline Gould
(Sir Stephen Runciman's cousin) for her delightful sketch of Garmisdale. Last, but by no means least, Virginia McKenna for writing the
Foreword.

But above all I want to thank Anne McNicol of Imprint for her
wonderful help in compiling this book and providing, with endless
patience, her skill, wisdom, spelling corrections and common sense
in keeping my feet at least almost on the ground!

FOREWORD

THIS IS A VERY PERSONAL STORY told with affection and with unusual attention to the details of everyday life, both present and past.

As I have not, as yet, visited Eigg, I cannot contribute my own feelings and experiences, but as a fond and enthusiastic visitor to the Western Highlands of Scotland, where each bay and each vista holds its own special magic, I can understand well Peta Orr's deep feelings for her second 'home'.

As the author says, there are many corners of Eigg that, even after forty years, she has yet to explore, but those she has visited and knows so well illuminate the main substance of her story which, for me, is of her friendships and relationships with the inhabitants of this little island.

She shares these friendships with us and the joys and griefs which so strongly bind people together. She allows us to glimpse a way of life with its own unique rhythm and space that city dwellers, pressured by technology and the demands of business and commerce, rarely have the fortune to experience.

Having finished the book I understand Peta Orr's joy that the islanders now own Eigg. There seems little doubt that they will cherish and protect it, and provide a safe haven for those of us who yearn to sit on the hills and gaze out to sea. Or dance the night away to the accordion or the pipes.

Virginia

Virginia McKenna
'Keep Wildlife in the Wild'

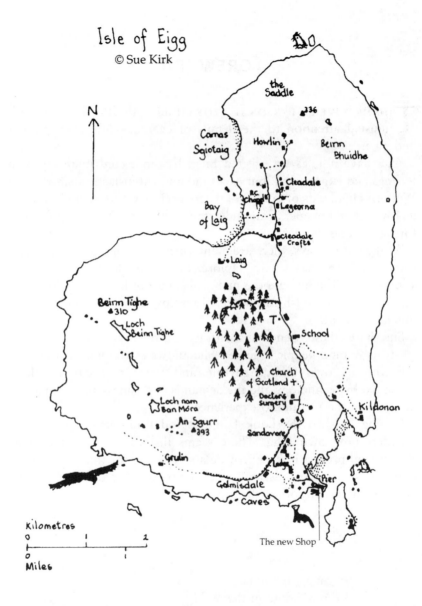

Isle of Eigg
© Sue Kirk

N

the Saddle

336

Camas Sgiotaig

Howlin

Beinn Bhuidhe

Cleadale

RC Chapel

Legeorna

Bay of Laig

Cleadale Crofts

Laig

School

Beinn Tighe
310

Loch Beinn Tighe

T.

Church of Scotland

Kildonan

Loch nam Ban Móra

Doctor's surgery

An Sgurr
393

Sandavore

Grulin

Galmisdale

Pier

Caves

Kilometres
0   1   2

Miles
0   1

The new Shop

1

What and Where is Eigg

Eigg is one of four islands in the Scottish Inner Hebrides, known as 'the Parish of the Small Isles'. The other three are Muck, to the south, Rhum and Canna to the west.

Eigg is five miles long by three miles wide. It lies south of the Isle of Skye and eight sea miles from Morar on the mainland. The Sgurr is the highest point, rising to 1,296 feet. This is very distinctive in shape, and makes Eigg instantly recognisable.

Who's who in this book:
The author with her daughters Jane and Rosie, Jean White and Peggy Kirk.

The author's children

Ian, Jane and Rosie
Ian is married to Rosie, and their children are Sophie, William and Katie.

Ian's sister Rosie is married to Rick; their children are Claudia and Tamsin.

Jane has two children, Lucy and Jack, and is divorced.

The children of Peggy and Donnie Kirk

Marie, Angus, Alastair, Fiona and D.J. (Donald Joseph)
Marie married Colin Carr.
Fiona married Mark Cherry.
Angus married Mairie (they are now separated).
Alastair married Sue, an English girl.
D.J. married Kay, also an English girl, from London.

2

EIGG: THE STORY OF ONE FAMILY'S LOVE AFFAIR WITH AN ISLAND

I am always asked "Why Eigg?" and what took us there
in the first place.
So – are you sitting comfortably?
Then I will begin.

MY HUSBAND, Bill, and I were married in 1956 in Holy Trinity, Brompton. It had been my own church and the Vicar remarked that it made a change to marry someone he knew! We had bought a small plot of land in Surrey. While our house was being built we shared a flat with John and Eve Dennison and their daughter, Arabella, in Oakwood Court by Holland Park.

Eve had gone to school in Edinburgh with a Violet Gowans. Violet had come to stay on the first stage of a round-the-world trip that was her 21st birthday present for her son, Fergus. John was Director of Music for the Arts Council, Eve worked for the BBC, Arabella was at boarding school and Fergus was staying with a friend. This meant that Violet and I were together all day. I missed the bustle of my training school, St Mary's Paddington, and Violet missed all her friends on Eigg, so we became firm friends. Also, I was able to dress her arm every day. Violet had had a nasty reaction to her smallpox vaccination. The last thing Violet said when we came to say goodbye was: "You must come to Eigg!"

So we did – for the next 40 years!

It was two years before we were able to cross over and stay at Kildonnan with Violet Gowans and her son Fergus, returning the following day. Before that, the service from Mallaig with the old *Loch Mor* was very infrequent. So for the first time we left our car at Mallaig and boarded the *Loch Mor* for the one and a half-hour

Angus, John and Simon loading goods into the Eigg ferry from the *Loch Mor.*

The Eigg ferry pulling away from the *Loch Mor* off Castle Island.

crossing to Eigg Harbour. Luckily it was a calm crossing as Bill was a dreadful sailor, and might never have gone again.

Caledonian MacBrayne own most of the boats on the West Coast of Scotland, and they sold us a ticket to Eigg Harbour. Note the word 'harbour' and not 'pier', since the water is not deep enough for the *Loch Mor* to berth at the pier. She stands off the island and waits for the Eigg ferry to meet her. When the little island ferry is

The Lodge and garden, designed by Sir Stephen Runciman after Tresco and Inverew gardens.

The Protestant Kirk.

The old shop.

tied up to her, any foot passengers leaving the island will board the
Loch Mor first; then the Royal Mail, diesel, messages and food for
the shop are loaded. Then it was our turn; a local cheerfully com-
mented that they hadn't dropped anyone yet! Two burly seaman
firmly get hold of you on either side and one moment you are on
the *Loch Mor* and the next you are in the ferry below. Fergus had
warned us not to jump in as we might go through the bottom of
the little boat! Luckily for us all was well, but we were all relieved
to see a new Eigg ferryboat the next year! The old *Loch Mor* sank
one day at the entrance to Mallaig harbour, thankfully with no
casualties.

Fergus was waiting for us on the pier. He had hired Dougie
MacKinnon, Eigg's taxi driver, to take us round the island. Wherever
you are on the island you can see the Sgurr, which is the highest
point on the island, the distinctive feature peculiar to Eigg. The
owner at the time was Lord Runciman, and as he was away we
drove through the grounds of the Lodge. It was and still is a lovely
garden, with several palm trees, a Brazilian flame tree and abundant
rhododendrons and azaleas. Eigg is a very fertile island washed by
the Gulf Stream. If you have enough shelter from the wind you can

'Old' Duncan Ferguson outside the priest's house.

grow anything on Eigg. The Lodge was built in 1930 and was a very attractive house. After the Lodge we set off to go to the other side of the island passing on our way Doctor MacLean's house. Dr MacLean was the doctor for the Small Isles; Eigg was fortunate that he lived with his wife on the island, he visited the other islands by boat. If the weather was bad the lifeboat would come over from Mallaig and take him. Very close to the Doctor's house was the Protestant Kirk. Unfortunately, the sermons were never less than two hours long, and I am ashamed to say that I never felt able to endure that. On our way to visit the other side of the island moorland stretched away on either side – to our left up to the Sgurr and to the right to the high ridge above Cleadale.

A little further on we came to the school. The children stay there until they are eleven years old, then they have to go to the mainland and live in hostels unless there are any relations to stay with. The Shop was just a short distance from the school, a corrugated iron hut without any water or electricity. Having passed it we came to the brow of a hill and our first sight of the most breathtakingly beautiful view stretched out before us across to the Isle of Rhum and the Cuillins on the Isle of Skye with Laig Bay in the foreground. It was a lovely sunny day and the sea sparkled with an intense blue reflected from the sky. Even after forty years I have still not seen anything to beat that view; on some days when it is very clear you can just see the Isle of Barra. Fergus pointed to a farmhouse nestling under some high cliffs by Laig Bay, with half a mile of silver sand. Fergus told us that it was Laig Farm and the farmer's wife Peggy Kirk ran it as a guesthouse – and that it was a good place for a family holiday.

We went down a very steep hill to the village of Cleadale where the crofters lived. We passed many attractive houses and Fergus also pointed out the Catholic Church amongst some trees with the Presbytery attached to it. Fergus told us that Duncan Ferguson and his wife Dolly lived there and looked after the church and any priests who came to stay. They were a delightful couple, loved and respected by everyone. A path ran down to the beach, past the church. We

Kildonnan.

Kildonnan: line drawing by Ronald Brett.

Howlin.

The Madonna from the Chapel in
Kildonnan.

The remains of the Chapel of St
Kildonnan and the Celtic Cross.

drove to the end of the road, where an imposing house by the name of Howlin stood. It was empty then, sometimes used for self-catering, and some years later a small group of breakaway monks lived there for a while. There was not time then to leave the taxi and walk across the fields to the famous Camus Sciotaig — 'the Singing Sands'. Fergus kept pointing to places we should visit if we came for a holiday. Dougie turned the taxi round and turned back but instead of taking the road down to the pier branched off left after the school and ran down to Kildonnan House, where Fergus was living with his mother.

Kildonnan was, and still is, a lovely house to stay in — it has a delightful welcoming feel. Even in the year 2000 there was no mains electricity on Eigg and in 1959 only the Lodge had a generator. Fergus looked after the oil lamps and washed the glasses every morning. I was worried about Ian as he always slept with a light on; he was

Inside the Kildonnan Chapel.

only two and a half years old then. I should not have worried – in June, it was light all night. The sitting room was on the first floor with a log fire burning. It had two large windows: from one you could see the mainland and from the other the pier and the Sgurr!

We could only stay one night as we had left Jane, who was a baby, with Bill's parents who lived in Learmonth Terrace in Edinburgh. The following morning Fergus had time before the boat came to show us the mound near the house, where Viking remains had been found. They had been taken to the museum of antiquities in Edinburgh. We have since seen them, but I feel it is sad they could not have been kept on Eigg. We also went up the hill behind the house to see the remains of the ruined chapel of Kildonnan. In Columba's time there was a St Donan who had 40 monks under him. One day while they were saying mass, Vikings or pirates – no one knows which – broke in to the chapel. St Donan asked if they could finish mass. They were told they could do so. Once they had finished mass, St Donan led the monks out of the chapel so that it was not defiled. They were all murdered.

Just by the chapel is the island's graveyard. The Catholics are buried near the chapel and the Protestants a little further away. Little did I know then that in years to come Bill and Fergus would lie next to each other in the Protestant part of that graveyard.

3

EARLY DAYS AT LAIG

L AIG FARM was – and still is – a large rambling farmhouse over 400 years old. It was a long time before the Kirks could afford a generator. Until they were able to have a generator Peggy washed everything by hand, using a glass rubbing board and a large mangle to ring out the washing. Her flat irons were heated on the stove. A little later she added an oven and grill run off Calor gas. Her fridge also ran off Calor gas very successfully. A coal and wood fire heated the guests' sitting room. Laig has three double bedrooms and one with three beds on the first floor. An extra loo and shower were added a lot later, otherwise there was only the bath and loo on the ground floor.

In the attic was one double bed and a single bed and, of course, cots.

The heart of the house was the kitchen. It was always warm and however wet clothes were they would always be dry in the morning on the large pulley.

The best evenings were the impromptu ceilidhs. Donnie Kirk, Peggy's husband, played the accordion superbly and taught Marie and Angus, their children; Hughie Cameron would sing, and Father Lennard would tell wonderful ghost stories very quietly, then clap loudly, and we would all jump out of our skins. In fact, one of Keith Schellenberg's daughters was convinced she had seen some ghosts, two men covered in white, wailing one dark evening.

They turned out to be the foresters, who came every year with bags of fertiliser for the trees. They always got covered in the stuff. They were most offended: "We were singing, not wailing!"

Father Lennard was in the Essex Regiment in the last war. He told us they had been under heavy shelling and when they went to look for one of the Junior Officers all they found was his foot. This was buried with full military honours and Father Lennard wrote an obituary for *The Times*. Some time later Father Lennard was touring

Father Lennard with Mairi
on her wedding day.

Father Lennard with Katy
Morag on a wet day.

a military hospital, and found the rest of the Officer sitting up in bed! "Thank you for my obituary," he said!

The other story occurred at the end of the war:

"I am the British Army"
by The Revd. Hugh Barrett Lennard, 15th August 1944

We had entered a little village called Esson after two days of close fighting. It was the Feast of the Assumption so we rang the bells of the Church and our Padre said Mass for the villagers.

My C.O. sent me on in a jeep, with a friendly driver, into 'No-Man's Land'. Unknown to us, the Germans had withdrawn in order to defend Falaise. We arrived about 6 a.m. to complete silence in an empty town – it was very eerie. I spotted a house with one word on it: 'Mairie'. I rang the bell and hammered on the door and an angry head wearing a nightcap appeared. "*Qui est là?*" he demanded furiously. For the only time in my life I was able to say: "*Je suis l'armée Britannique*" – the nearest British troops were five miles away. It is not often one can make a claim like that! Very reasonably he then enquired "*Ou sont les autres?*"

Much rejoicing and wine in abundance followed. When I finally got back to make my report to the C.O. it was not all that intelligible! It was still only 9 a.m. in the morning.

The evening after Helen was found (see pp. 34 and 35) was one of the best. Relief and euphoria added to the delight of the evening. The usual crowd in the kitchen was swollen by all sorts of people who had been searching for Helen. I remember one couple who had only landed with their canoe to get fresh water and had joined the search. They had 'canoed' down from St Kilda. They had lots of stories. One night they had gone into a sea loch. It was a very dark night, with no moon or stars. They saw a bulky shape floating through the gloom. First they thought it must be a seal. Then 'it' hailed them – "Hi". There had been a very good party. This chap fell in, stoned out of his mind – wearing a souwester and 'oily' coat. The air had got inside and acted as a life jacket and he was floating happily along with the tide, rather like Eeyore in *Winnie the Pooh*.

They took him into town and landed him on the beach. They suspected he would not have remembered anything the next morning.

———————

Haymaking in those days was very labour intensive – no machinery at all. It was a hot summer and Bill and I took on a field to turn the hay by hand. We were young and foolish and kept slipping into the sea and back to the haymaking – we suffered with severe sunburn. We were thrilled to hear that Donnie had managed to get hold of a 'Woofeler' the following year.

———————

Although Donnie realised they needed the money from visitors, he did not like it. He had as little to do with them as possible. Peggy told me he often saw people in Peggy MacKinnon's shop and asked who they were, only to be told they were his guests! Perhaps because he realised that Bill really meant it when he offered help, that was the beginning of a very close relationship that lasted until Donnie's untimely death. Donnie even brought Peggy down to stay with us. He was a very special man. You felt he could do anything if he put his hand to it. Noel Banks, in his book *Six Inner Hebrides* dedicated the book to Donnie and referred to him as "the complete Islander", and he was – crofter, farmer and fisherman; the first to turn to in trouble of any kind. Whatever he did he did well. Marie Carr's husband, Colin, reminds me of him often. He sheared all his sheep without the electric shears they have today. The wool was sent away and came back as lovely blankets or knitting wool in the colour and ply that Peggy needed.

Peggy and I also became lifelong friends, with only three months between our ages.

———————

Like all the West Coast Islanders, Peggy used vegetables – except for potatoes; they were served separately – only for soup, not as a side dish, and would give her guests a whole leg of lamb to carve as much as they liked. I have never found any potatoes to beat the ones Donnie grew.

Donnie had a sturdy boat, safe enough for the dangerous waters round the islands. The lobsters were very hard work. I used to hear Donnie go out very early in the morning to check the pots, and again late in the evening. Occasionally he would put a line across the bay at night and in the morning there would be an amazing assortment of fish. That was the only time I was 'squeamish' – he brought some of the skate in straight out of the sea, skinned it and cut it up. The pieces were jumping about on the plate!

Peggy would not eat mackerel; she said it was scavenger fish and she would not dream of giving it to her visitors. It was only good enough for bait. In the end we persuaded her to give it just to us. She picked a fat one up. It was shining fresh – straight out of the sea. Taking a sharp knife she cut a chunk from both sides and threw the rest away. Then it was rolled in oatmeal and fried – and was wonderful.

4

GRADUAL CHANGES

WHEN WE ARRIVED on Eigg, Peggy and I would enjoy visiting the other crofters for a good gossip. The kettle would be simmering on the hob and we would be offered a cup of tea and 'a piece'. Over the years the 'tea' has mostly changed to coffee. In the 50s the women on the island hardly drank alcohol at all. They smoked a lot. In the 90s the young people would not dream of inviting their friends to dinner (that was unheard of in their childhood) without offering them wine.

Granny Kirk was content with her black stove and, indeed, produced some wonderful food from it. Her grandchildren have microwaves (when the generator is working) and electric mixers, televisions and mobile phones. Laura Ashley catalogues produce pretty curtains and matching bedlinen.

Mail order was a wonderful boon and blessing to the islanders. Fort William was the nearest shopping place and was fairly limited in what it had to offer. It was mainly aimed at the tourist, otherwise you had to go to Inverness or Glasgow. That involved being away for some considerable time. Several women ran the catalogues and made a little pin money. Not only could you order pretty well most things, but they were delivered to the island as well. In Laig, for instance, all the kitchen cupboards and tiles for the bathroom came through a catalogue.

Peggy's cooking became more varied. She had the Scottish Rurals cook book (from the Scottish W. I.) and I was forced to buy my own after all the tasty meals kept appearing, including vegetarian or side dishes.

From the two cars when we arrived, more and more ancient cars started to appear. The dreadful roads and the salt meant their life on the island was very short and they joined the little graveyards round the island. What to do with them became a problem. Some were dumped in the sea but that was not doing the sea much good.

Granny Kirk's stove.

A 'dead car', used as a greenhouse.

A car graveyard.

It was expensive to return them to the mainland. Unlike Iona, Inverness County Council did not help with refuse disposal. One of the cars came in handy and was used for a little greenhouse which produced some good cuttings, and the hens lived in a Rolls Royce van!

One of the gigantic changes was the installation of the ugly Telephone Exchange. Before it arrived, phoning Eigg was an experience. If you were wise you made yourself comfortable with a few sandwiches and thermos of coffee and a lot of patience! Having given the telephone number, Eigg 37 – or Eigg 2, for the Gowans in Kildonnan – you settled down to hear a lot of whistling noises and eventually, "You are through to Glasgow, caller." More time and atmospheric noises, and you were through to Oban; then Fort William and finally, feeling decidedly travel-weary, you were through to Mallaig and, at last (via Peggy MacKinnon if it was day time) you heard Peggy Kirk's voice saying "Oh, hello, Peta." Peggy always answered the phone in English but would instantly break into the Gaelic if needed. Peggy was born on Uist – like Barra, a Catholic and Gaelic speaking island.

Garmisdale.

It was such a pity when the telephone no longer went through Peggy MacKinnon. All the colour went out of the calls.

Fergus Gowans' mother, Violet, had been given the lease of Kildonnan for her lifetime. The day she died he was given notice to quit Kildonnan by Mr Evans' factor. For some years, until he finally bought a piece of church land and built a bungalow, he lived all over the island, especially in Garmisdale. I remember he was showing us round the house and I asked what all the saucers were for in the bedrooms. "Rat poison," said Fergus!

Anyway, this particular year no one seemed to know where he was. I had a brainwave and got through to Peggy MacKinnon and said: "Please could you put me through to Fergus?" This she did at once! She always knew where everyone was.

The 'Finger of God' Rock, Eigg looking down on the village of Cleadale and over to the Isle of Rhum.

5

EXPEDITIONS

FERGUS GOWANS always 'master-minded' and led all our expeditions to explore Eigg. Eigg may sound small but there are still places I have not reached yet. Fergus helped with the little ones and would stride through the heather, kilt swinging, with a youngster under his arm.

Fergus would also add a touch of luxury to the ample packed lunch Peggy had prepared. The Gowans received a delivery from Harrods or Fortnum & Mason every month!

THE SGURR

The Sgurr is the largest lump of columnar basalt in the British Isles. It screams to be climbed. It also gives the island its name. Looking

View of the Sgurr and Laig Bay with the Singing Sands in the foreground; taken from the ridge.

at Eigg from the mainland the Sgurr's outline resembles the shape of
a 'notch'. 'Eigg' is Norse for notch.

One day in 1966, guided by Fergus, we set off to climb it. Behind
Laig are steep cliffs but there is an easy path that zigzags up the side
of part of it. To my mind it is the last 'easy' bit of the journey. You
end up at the top in rough moorland, dotted with small lochs full
of trout. There are lots of boggy bits, usually marked by the white,
fluffy, cotton grass. My daughter Rosie was three then. She is not
the youngest to have climbed the Sgurr but she is the youngest to
have done it the long way and, stubbornly refusing all sensible shoes,
in 'flip flops'!

There is a much easier and quicker route up from the other end
of the island but Fergus was determined we should do things
properly.

I am the original wimp and found the rough scrub very hard going
– not so Rosie, who was always well ahead. The Kirk children had
done it before and made light work of it. When we finally reached
the top I had to admit it was worth it. It was a lovely clear day and
the view was breathtaking. On the left you could see the lovely little
Isle of Muck. If you were lucky you could see Barra in the Outer
Hebrides in the far distance. To the west you had a superb view of
Rhum. Eigg is fertile because it was a volcanic island. The volcano
all those years ago was on Rhum. Viewed from the top of the Sgurr
you can see where the volcano must have been. You could also see
the little lochans we had passed on the way up – one is supposed
to be haunted!

To the left you can see the length of the Ridge of Eigg and over
to the mainland, Morar, and Ardnamurchan. To the north west you
are looking at the Isle of Skye with the beautiful Cuillin Hills. Fergus
dug out a rusty tin with a notebook inside for all the names of those
who reached the summit. Not surprisingly, it disappeared for ever
in the winter gales.

We then dropped down the 'short' way, past Garmisdale and
Sandavore to the road, and back by the short cut to Laig, tired but
happy.

CAMUS SCIOTAIG – THE SINGING SANDS

One of our favourite expeditions – and one of the shorter ones – was to the next bay along from Laig: the famous Singing Sands. You can get to it two ways. You can follow an ebbing tide and scramble over the rocks – it really is a scramble but great fun. Or you can have a gentle walk through the village of Cleadale to the end of that road to Howlin, then cut across the fields and find the path down to the beach. You must stick to the path because there is a sheer drop under the cliff.

Once on the Sands you have to find some dry sand. Some years there is lots of sand – other years hardly any; it is one of the mysteries of the beach. The sand disappears in the winter and comes back in a different place each summer. If you 'scuff' your feet in the dry sand it will squeak rather than 'sing'. The sound is the same as when you tread on thick snow for the first time. The sand in the little

The Singing Sands.

beach next to it looks exactly the same but will not squeak. The sea is much colder here for swimming. In Laig Bay I wait for the tide to go miles out then, when it comes back over the warm sand, it is very pleasant indeed for swimming.

The rock pools between the two bays are wonderful. Battered by the winter storms they also change shape and character. One summer there was a really large pool, quite deep and warm, of course, in the sun. We taught Marie to swim in it.

THE PUFFER

The expedition to the 'Puffer' was the one I least enjoyed and only really accomplished once. The children loved it. Now nothing remains of the brave little boat that used to take coal to the islands and was shipwrecked on the north coast of Eigg in 1954.

We went past Howlin House, where some breakaway Anglican monks were living, and over the 'Saddle'. By that time it was lunchtime and we enjoyed Peggy's sandwiches, cake and fruit, and Fergus' contribution from Fortnums, and got strength for the next part of the journey. That was the bit I did not like. The path crossed the top of a steep slope of shale; the path had only been made by the sheep and in places was missing altogether. The shale was always slipping under your feet and I hated it. Anyway, once past there it was easy going to the Puffer.

At that time there was quite a lot of it left and all the children loved it. Marie and Jane climbed inside and with great glee used the loo. The chain actually still flushed the toilet to the children's delight and much giggling.

Some years later I had refused to negotiate the shale cliff and was happily lounging in the heather, enjoying the scent of wild thyme in the sun, when I heard singing. I was sure it was the children returning. It was the seals singing on the rocks below – lovely.

OTTERS

I have always loved otters but only ever seen one and that did not count as it was tame-ish! She was called Tibby and lived with Archie the boatman near the pier.

One year I had made the mistake of getting a catering sized tin of instant coffee. I never did that again as it was stale long before we had ploughed our way through it. However I entered a competition run by the manufacturers. You had as many tries as there were ounces on the label – I had a lot! I won first prize: a movie camera, film, projector, screen and book. As this was obviously bulky I wondered how it would arrive. It never occurred to me they would bring it themselves. One morning we were having breakfast and a large van from the coffee company drew up outside.

Anyway, that year only we took it to Eigg and it came with us when we went to meet Tibby. Bill was waiting with camera at the ready. Round the corner she came. Bill got a brief shot of her, then

Archie with Tibby, the otter that went to Gavin Maxwell at Camusfearna.

Archie and his tame otter on Eigg.

she bit Archie and Bill stopped filming. I was very annoyed and asked him why he had stopped filming. Bill said he felt it was bad manners to film Archie dripping with blood. I thought it would have come out beautifully in colour!

Archie got very bad arthritis and could no longer care for Tibby. She went to Gavin Maxwell and is mentioned in one of his books, *Raven Seek Thy Brother*.

One summer Peggy and I were driven mad by successive guests coming back to Laig full of the otters they had seen. We spent every evening sitting quietly, being eaten alive by midges, but no otters. So we decided that we had both seen Tibby and that would have to last us!

Granny Kirk's Picnic

Granny Kirk (Donnie's mother) was a small, neat little lady, solid as a rock and deeply loved by everyone who knew her. She was a wonderful help to Peggy and I can still see her sitting upright in Laig kitchen – always with her spotless apron on, because she never stopped working. Papa Kirk also was a lovely old man who worked his croft. We felt privileged to know them both. Granny Kirk had an old-fashioned black range; this heated water and the house and was used for all the cooking. There was always a kettle simmering on the hob, ready to give any caller a 'strupag' (cup of tea and a 'piece' that could be cake, biscuit or freshly baked bread with butter and jam). That accompanied the welcome any caller would receive.

We were so honoured: Granny Kirk had never been further afield than Glasgow, so it was very brave of her to come south to stay with us in Surrey, bringing Marie and Angus. It was very special and wonderful also to have the children – it was the Christmas holidays. The children were not used to the traffic: there were only two cars on Eigg – and they met head on! South-east England even then had more than anywhere else in Britain. Angus disappeared on Ian's bicycle – I was sick with worry. He returned without mishap but I got Bill to put the bike in the attic. No generators meant no freezers; this meant no icecream, so they made up for lost time. I never had to think what to get for dessert!

While they were there we had a New Year's Eve party. We took the carpet up for dancing. Granny Kirk was very light on her feet and capable of dancing the most elaborate Highland dances. Donnie had taught both Angus and Marie to play the accordion; Ian had a friend, Andrew Fowler-Watt, at his prep school, Brambletye, who also played the accordion. Andrew started the evening off with an eightsome reel and 'Strip the Willow': he played very fast. Angus and Marie took turns to play at a much slower pace. Those two were still playing at 2 a.m. They had been taught to 'pace' themselves. All Eigg ceilidhs lasted till dawn!

Granny Kirk waited to say 'thankyou' until next summer when she invited us to a picnic on Laig Beach. I will never forget it – it was wonderful. Granny had cooked a clouty dumpling: this is a Christmas cake-type recipe, boiled in a cloth. It came down to the beach on a plate. The teapot came too, with its cosy, as well as other goodies. The dumpling was cut up and the Orrs and the Kirks fell on it. In minutes there was not a crumb left. It was quite delicious. It was such a happy afternoon.

Bill and I managed to visit Granny Kirk in Fort William just before she died. She could not speak but squeezed our hands. We were heartbroken when she died.

THE CAVES

Massacre Cave:
I only visited the Massacre Cave once, in 1975. To me it was a Middle Ages Auschwitz-type gas chamber – and claustrophobic. In the 16th century there were many 'bloody' feuds between the Clans. The one in question was between the MacDonalds of Eigg and MacLeods of Dunvegan in Skye. There were dreadful atrocities. To be honest, they were as bad as one another!

It was started by Clanranald (MacDonald of Eigg) insulting MacLeod of Dunvegan (Isle of Skye). He was married to MacLeod's daughter and he threw her aside and got someone else. The MacLeods retaliated by beheading the entire crew of a Clanranald galley blown onto the coast of Harris by a storm. Another storm forced the MacLeods to take shelter on Castle Island, Eigg. The entire inhabitants of Eigg then descended on them and killed all except the leaders. They broke all their bones and turned them loose in their boat without oars or rudder to drive and starve. However the current took them back to Dunvegan in Skye! The MacLeods sent a revenge party. The Eigg people saw them coming and all except one old lady hid in Uamh Fraing, the Massacre Cave, for three days. They then sent out a scout. It had been snowing. The MacLeods saw the scout and followed his steps back to the cave. They made a fire at the entrance and everyone inside died from suffocation, leaving the one old lady, found wandering the other side of the island. They burnt her house and destroyed all means of her food. This is the merest outline. You will find the full story, and much more history of Eigg, going back to 6000 BC, in Camille Dressler's book *Eigg, The Story of an Island*.

The cave has a narrow entrance, but once inside it is vast. I believe that even with powerful flares no one has seen the roof.

The Massacre Cave.

The Cathedral Cave.

Cathedral Cave:
Only a few yards away is a beautiful cave. It got its name not only
from its dimensions, but also because at the very back is a boulder,
convenient for an altar. When the Catholics were prohibited from
saying Mass they were able to go there in secret. Now it is used for
barbecues or just keeping out of the rain.

6

THE GOLDEN EAGLE

FOR YEARS I WOULD TRY and convince myself that every buzzard
I saw was an eagle! Colin, being a shepherd, knew exactly where
the eagle was; he very kindly piled us all into his Landrover one
evening and off we went. He drove as far as he was able, then we
walked for another 20 minutes. Colin then made us all lie down in
the heather some way from her nest. We were chatting away when
suddenly Colin said, "Shush. The crows are making a noise; something is coming." I thought that was a lovely piece of country lore.
Sure enough, seconds later there she was. Once you have seen an
eagle you never confuse them with a buzzard again! I had a powerful
telephoto lens that picked up the little white blob that was her chick.
We did not want to get too close to the nest. It was thrilling seeing
the mother soaring up in the thermals. Colin tells me she has come
back each year and produced more chicks.

Sea Eagles have been introduced onto Rhum; they sometimes fly
over to Eigg but do not nest there. There was some talk of putting
wolves on Rhum – that would keep the tourists down! So far they
have stuck to deer and ponies. The whole island is owned by Nature
Conservancy.

The dramatic shapes of mountains and valleys on Rhum are caused
by the volcanic origins of the island.

You will find the worst "cleggs" (type of horse flies) in Scotland
on Rhum. The only time I went there I smothered myself in anti-
insect lotion, forgetting I might need to find a convenient bush, so
I had a ring of bites all round my waist!

7

HELEN

It had been one of those golden days you can get on the west coast. At 10 p.m. the telephone rang. Had any of us seen Helen Nimmo Smith? Helen was 16 and had been coming for years with her mother, Anne, and family, plus all their dogs and cats, for six months. She was a great bird-watcher and used to going off by herself for long periods. Her mother did not worry until it had become very late. No one had seen her. On the mainland that would not have been so remarkable, but on the island you were hard-pressed to go anywhere without someone seeing you and remembering, especially as everyone knew Helen so well.

Peggy and I stayed with the children. Donnie Kirk and Bill were out all night with all the other men on the Island. Bill told us later that Donnie had run up the Sgurr – no sign of her anywhere! I remember Donnie saying that if she had gone down Grulin we might never find her.

At first light an RAF Shackleton arrived and 'wheeled' low over the island. It felt sinister and made us realise how serious the situation was. We did not dare wave in case the pilot thought we had found her.

This was followed by two helicopters, one RAF and one Naval. They stayed all day. By this time we had all joined in the search. I remember finding a place for a quick 'wee' very difficult because, instead of the deserted moorland it usually was, just as you found a convenient bush, along came a helicopter! On one occasion I had not noticed it on the other side of a hillock until it rose up. Poor chaps probably in the same dire need!

The lifeboat arrived from Mallaig. It went round the island very slowly with the crew's glasses trained on the rocks.

Then the Press arrived! A light aircraft landed on Laig Beach. Until then I had thought of Eigg as a remote island!

In the late afternoon we received word to stop searching and rest. Tracker dogs were coming from Glasgow. They got airsick in a plane so were coming by boat. We were all to go to a field near Sandavore at 6 p.m. to continue the search with the dogs.

We arrived with others in time to see one of the Press wrap a £5 note round his film and hand it to a helicopter pilot so that his film would be first in Glasgow for the early papers. Then I saw Helen's mother, Anne Nimmo Smith, get in and the helicopter took off for Fort William. They had found her!

Later we heard that the helicopter pilots had said they would do one more circuit of the island and then leave it to the people on the ground and the tracker dogs.

Suddenly, one airman saw her head move. Even so, they had to circle a few times to find her. She had indeed fallen down on the black rocks at Grulin that Donnie had feared so much, but also she was wearing black clothes. Fergus had been immediately above her at 3 a.m. but, of course, she was unconscious. What saved her life was the weather – or should I say the lack of it? There was no wind or rain and it was pleasantly warm all night.

The yellow helicopter can be seen lifting off, taking Helen to hospital in Fort William.

8

THE SUMMER OF THE BOBBIN DINGHY

I N 1970 WE BOUGHT a 7ft dinghy called the *Bobbin* – great for rowing; pretty hopeless for sailing. This came with us to Eigg: on the roof rack; inside the guard's van; onto the ferry, Caledonian MacBrayne's *Loch Mor*, without an eyebrow lifted; into Eigg ferry and then via Donnie's tractor to Laig. The children had a whale of a time in it. Bill sailed it round to the Singing Sands one afternoon. I rashly offered to sail it back with Angus. It simply would not 'go about'! I think in the end we stayed on the same tack until we were level with Laig and Angus swam ashore towing it!

On our way south torrential rain had washed away the track north of Stirling where we were joining the motor-rail. A dour Scots railway guard looked at the dinghy and said, without a glimmer: "I see you have alternative transport."

The *Bobbin*.

Bill in the Wayfarer.

While Rosie was at home we kept the *Bobbin*. Bill and I had joined Weir Wood Sailing Club and raced from October to March. I loved our dark blue sails but we had to change them for white ones – blue was too conspicuous as we always came last! Not only was it safe for Rosie to sail on the reservoir but she came in useful on windless days by towing us to the start line. However, the *Bobbin* had to go in the end.

We had taken it down to Itchenor in Chichester Harbour and I had gone out with Iain Radford, a more than competent sailor (he had helped crew the *Sapper* boat in the Fastnet race). The *Bobbin* capsized. We managed to 'right' it again but it then floated under the water. (We had a spirited correspondence with the makers afterwards and the buoyancy is now improved). I was always taught never to let go of the boat. I was so near the bows I was convinced that just one stroke and I would be at the bows and could get the boat's head to wind – and upright. There is an 8-knot tide running at Itchenor – one stroke and I was on my way to the Isle of Wight! My danger then was from the propellers of the many kind motor boats who speedily checked my progress to the open sea.

After that we sold her. When we handed her over to the new owners we begged them never to sail her in tidal waters and – to salve my conscience – I gave them a lifejacket!

We then bought a decent boat – a second-hand Wayfarer. I loved her, although her name, *Solea*, left a lot to be desired – I was happyish with it until I found it meant 'Flat Fish', so for ever after I referred to it as The Wayfarer.

9

DRAMA – FIRE AND WATER: TWO NEAR DISASTERS

WE ONLY TOWED our caravan up to Arisaig once. Arisaig is on the mainland, opposite Eigg. The caravan was perfect as a base when visiting Ian at Oundle. There was only one small hotel and 800 boys. On Speech Day all the parents were allowed to park their caravans on the games field and we had bread, milk and papers delivered and could use the showers. However, our caravan was far too small for a family holiday. The children had to sleep in a tent and at Ballahulish it rained as only the West Coast knows how, so we all had to squeeze inside.

We had booked into a camp site near Arisaig, run by a lovely lady who had a cow called Lugs. Not far from our caravan was another with a large family and a dog. The wife had stayed behind to prepare the supper and all the rest had gone fishing. The wife decided to heat the oil for the chips, then turn off the gas before she went to collect the others. Off she went with the dog. She had not turned off the gas! That caravan was burnt to the ground in ten minutes flat. There was an explosives expert staying on the site. He made us get back a long way in case the gas cylinder exploded: in fact, because it was turned on, it was not under pressure. What did explode, making the whole thing look like November 5th, were all the tins! They went in all directions like rockets.

We all suffered a degree of shock – apart from anything else because of the speed that it happened. Luckily the wind blew the flames away from the other caravans.

That poor family – you can imagine their state when they arrived back. At least there had been no loss of life (the wife had nearly left the dog behind). The fire engine turned up in time to damp it down.

We managed to squeeze them into our caravan. Bill used to pass the Scout Shop in Victoria on his way to work and had bought some packs of food to which you only had to add water. I found one of Chicken Supreme for ten people, added some fresh mushrooms, and it went round nicely. At the same time, sitting rigidly upright on one of the beds, was the Mallaig Policeman, taking notes – he thought it was arson.

The family wanted to get in their car and drive straight home. We persuaded them not to as they were suffering from severe shock. The lady who owned the site put them in an empty caravan and we lent them everything they needed. It was not until the next day when we said goodbye that I noticed the little girl had one hand missing.

The reason we had brought the caravan and camped over night was because some close friends of ours, Iain and Jane Radford with two of their four children, Giles and Pelly – short for Petronella – had volunteered to tow up our Wayfarer. They stayed the night before the trip over to Eigg in a hired caravan (Iain told me, in damp blankets!). Jane and I saw them off, then took the children over on

The caravan in flames.

the *Sheerwater*. We had an 'interesting' trip as it was blowing a gale and waves were breaking over the bow of the ship. Still, the *Sheerwater* – a converted minesweeper – is a very safe boat and had there been any danger Murdoch Grant, the owner, would not have gone.

The following is based on Major Iain Radford's account of their crossing to Eigg ...
They launched by a long, shallow beach, waved off by their respective families. It seemed forever before they were able to start sailing. (Iain was extremely fed up because he had bought a new pair of trousers especially for the holiday and tore them on the way to the boat!).

To start with the weather was not too bad. The problem was that although they had a good compass the mist had come down and they could not see Eigg. The wind got up and Bill changed to storm sails; they considered reefing them. Meanwhile the mist became thicker. Although they were in no immediate danger, the mist made it almost impossible to identify the light they could see on their right. It could have been Skye or the extreme end of the Isle of Muck. They could only press on and hope it was Skye! Suddenly there was a brief break in the clouds. Bill recognised Rhum, with its distinctive valley between two hills. They were still north of Eigg. Once they got into the shelter of Eigg the huge waves lessened and they sailed into Eigg Harbour. Iain told me it had been very hard work indeed. If they had not been young and very fit the outcome could have been very different. They were met on the pier by an interested group of kilted gentry, led by Fergus Gowans, who were on their way back from the Highland Games. They all produced their hip flasks: it was the first time Iain had met "a wee dram"!

When Donnie saw the Wayfarer he said he had no idea it was such a large dinghy. A Wayfarer is 17ft long and as stable as they come. Wayfarers have sailed to Norway and the Fair Isles.

Meanwhile, back in the kitchen at Laig Farm, it had been a desperately worrying time for Jane and me. Peggy had a 'yacht boy' radio so that Donnie could speak to her from his boat. Donnie was speaking in Gaelic but he might just as well have spoken in English. We could tell from the tone of his voice how concerned he was. Donnie had gone looking for them in his boat but, of course, could not see a thing because of the mists. Also, Bill did not have a reflector on his mast so it would not have been picked up by Donnie's radar. He admitted afterwards that he had feared the worst.

Ironically, when it came to sailing back, Iain and Bill had a boiling hot day with just enough wind to fill the spinnaker. All they had to do was to lie back and sunbathe. Iain said it was the longest spinnaker run of his entire life!

Meanwhile, we had the Wayfarer to enjoy on the island. It was good to have room for all the children – except Pelly Radford. Pelly was, and still is, a very exceptional girl. Blind from birth she has a wonderful capacity for enjoying life: she also has very definite likes and dislikes. Boats – especially anything less than a cross-channel steamer – are definitely not for Pelly. That was why, one lovely summer day, having walked to the Singing Sands, Pelly firmly started to walk back to Laig Farm. Bill and Jane went with her and Iain and I took Giles Radford and the Kirk and Orr children to Laig Bay in the Wayfarer.

As we arrived in Laig Bay, Helen's mother, Anne Nimmo Smith, arrived from Muck, in the other direction. She had a folkboat – ideal for those waters, especially if you wanted to fish, as the stay sail kept the boat head to wind. Anne had very kindly made the effort to come and see us. She dropped anchor and got into a rubber dinghy to come ashore. There was a loud hissing noise and the dinghy started to sink. Iain immediately sailed over and took her on board. Anne has always been a 'large' lady. Once Iain had landed on the beach he shouted "Out"; this was for me and the children. Unfortunately Anne thought this meant her – with disastrous results.

For years Anne had come up from Oxford – with all the children, retriever dogs and cats – and spent three months on Eigg, often in Tigh-a-Bhlar. I remember that one boiling hot day she had walked to the shop; by the time she had walked back again she was expiring with the heat. She walked down the road, across the beach and straight into the sea – kilt and all. Very sensible!

They moved to the Isle of Muck for holidays and eventually to retire. We used to see her when we went over to Muck. I went once or twice with Donnie, taking sacks of his wonderful potatoes. There was no pier in those days and it was a slippery business clambering over the seaweed.

We enjoyed having the Radfords; it was wonderful for Bill to have the company of another chap to go on really long walks and climbs with, without having a child to carry. Jane Radford and I had been friends from the day we moved into our new house and she came down the drive pushing Giles (then about seven months old – the same age as Ian). The boys went to Brambletye together and met up again at Sandhurst.

10

Eigg School

THE SCHOOL is situated in the middle of the island. The teacher lives in the building. The electricity came from a generator, except for a short period when Inverness County Council erected a windmill. It cost £3,000. After it blew down in a gale it was not replaced.

Children stay at this school until they are 11 years old. Then they have to leave the Island. In Marie's time they had to go to Fort William. Unless they had relatives in Fort William they had to live in a hostel. There were too many children to receive personal care and many children were unhappy, especially as they often only

The School.

managed one trip home during the term. Understandably this often resulted in the parents leaving Eigg. They did not always return.

Things are easier now. There is a Secondary School at Mallaig and it is easier to get back to the island, especially in the season when the *Sheerwater* is running.

Gaelic is taught in the school but only Peggy and her generation speak the language. Peggy was born on South Uist – a Gaelic-speaking island to this day. Peggy's daughter Marie can understand Gaelic and write it but speaks only English.

11

The Manse

WHEN WE FIRST WENT to Eigg a full-time Minister lived in the Manse with his wife who provided bed and breakfast. I gather she was not very generous with helpings – one piece of bread was normal. I asked one guest how he was getting on. He was very tactful and said, "She is very economical!"

The Manse has a wonderful position with glorious views over to the mainland. When Keith Schellenberg sold Eigg he kept the Manse. Sadly it is beginning to fall down from neglect. It is a shame, as it would make a lovely house for self-catering. Keith has only come back once and is not likely to spend any money on it.

The Manse.

12

ISLANDERS AND OTHER FRIENDS

FERGUS AND LESLIE GOWANS

Violet Gowans died in London in 1964, nursed by a delightful New Zealand nurse, Leslie. Violet had phoned me shortly before she died. She told me she longed to go back to Eigg to die but no one would let her go.

One good thing came from Violet's last illness: Fergus married Leslie. Leslie was a great asset to Eigg from the word 'go' – she was quiet, very kind and tactful, and was accepted by the islanders because she fitted in so well. It was also useful having another trained nurse on the island. She kept a special eye on all the old folk and the children.

Fergus had been a bachelor for a long while and was not all that

Bill with Fergus and Leslie Gowans.

Leslie Gowans with her geese.

easy to live with. Bill and I went to their reception in the Caledonian Club in London. Fergus had given Leslie a very long (floor-length) white mock rabbit coat. They had seen it in the window of Harrods, and Fergus went in and bought it. It was the only one, so Fergus made them take it off the model. Considering Fergus had lived almost all his life on Eigg it is hard to imagine when he thought Leslie would wear it again! It brought to mind one Easter on Eigg.

Poor Mrs Smith, Commander Smith's wife, was more at home in a Sussex town than on an island. She came to church one Easter Sunday dressed entirely in white from her parasol down to her shoes.

Leslie loved Eigg and its people and was very happy for many years. She kept geese and had a ginger kitten called Little Growl. She was an excellent cook. Instead of bread she made a delicious, very large, scone every day. She was a keen gardener and she joined in with all the island's activities.

Sadly Fergus died at the early age of 45, in hospital, after a long illness. Leslie stayed on for several years after Fergus' death.

However, her mother was still alive, and eventually she returned to New Zealand, where she is still nursing part-time. She was, and still is, greatly missed.

DONNIE AND PEGGY KIRK, AND DONNIE'S BROTHER FRANKIE

One Easter holiday we were shocked to get a phonecall from Peggy Kirk. Donnie had terminal cancer of the stomach. He seemed so strong and vibrant it did not seem possible he could be dying. The island could not do without him – it seemed so unfair. Keith Schellenberg had not long taken over ownership of Eigg. Peggy will always be grateful to him. He flew Donnie home to Eigg in his private plane so, instead of dying in a Glasgow hospital, Donnie's last days were in sight and sound of the sea, surrounded by his family and friends. Father Lennard had got leave to come up from Brompton Oratory and said Mass in Donnie's bedroom, with all his family and

In the kitchen at Laig Farm.
By the door: Rosie Orr and Sue Browning holding Pippo.
Front, left to right: Chrissie Cameron (Donnie's sister), Frankie Kirk (Donnie's brother), Peggy and Donnie Kirk.

Marie, John and Maggie playing for a Ceilidh.

friends, every night. Bill was heartbroken – they had been so close: "We must go and say goodbye," he said. We got as far as Mallaig. The weather was atrocious (it was the year the *Compass Rose* sank without trace).

Mallaig harbour was full of boats that had run for shelter. Nothing was moving: when we ventured out for some fresh air the wind flattened us against the wall. It had been snowing as well. Bill was worried that he would not get back through Glencoe and the passes would close up with snow. We all went to the telephone to say goodbye and explain we had to get back while we could. Before I could say a word, Peggy said, "Please can you come? Mary has collapsed." Mary Campbell had earned her Burma Star as an Army Nursing Sister. After the war, instead of taking life easily, she had been a District Nurse in Glasgow's Gorbels. She was now long past retiring age.

So Bill took Ian and Rosie and set off home while he could; Jane and I waited. The next day the weather relented enough for the *Loch*

Dougie MacKinnon.

Mor to sail. I fell on the way to the boat. It was so cold I did not feel it until I got into the warm kitchen at Laig and saw the blood. Mary dressed it for me. Donnie was very weak by now and in a lot of pain. Dr MacLean and I did our best to keep the pain within reasonable limits. It seemed strange giving injections by candlelight at night. It was bitterly cold – very unusual for Eigg (because of the Gulf Stream), with frequent showers of snow. It was lovely having Jane with me – she was able to keep us cheerful and even made us laugh sometimes. Jane and I would go for little walks delivering milk. We had a welcome wherever we went but most people would dissolve into tears. Donnie was deeply loved.

It was quite a relief to visit Julian Ward. Julian was equally fond of Donnie but he was not an islander, so not so much emotionally involved. Julian used to come most years with his friend, Richard Beeby, until Richard married Sue. Richard's mother, Cass, also loved

Eigg and always stayed at Laig Farm with Peggy. Julian now lives
on the Isle of Harris. Donnie's son D. J. (Donald Joseph) was only
a baby so sadly cannot remember his father. Alastair was confirmed
in his father's bedroom.

Father Lennard had to get back to Brompton Oratory. He very
kindly took Jane south with him. Years later he took part in Jane's
wedding service.

I had to leave, sadly, about a week before Donnie died. Frankie,
Donnie's brother, took me to Mallaig in Donnie's boat. As we sailed
into Mallaig Harbour the only London train of the day was leaving.
My heart sank! Frankie shouted something in Gaelic – we piled into
a taxi, which chased the train and stopped it where it crossed the
road at Morar. It is a long way up without a platform! Once inside
I collapsed in a heap in a corner and turned to thank the guard. To
my amazement he said: "It was the least we could do for you." I
had forgotten that everyone knows everything on the West Coast.
His kindness released the floodgates and for the first time I broke
down and wept.

George Walker

Donnie had been in the Merchant Navy with a Glaswegian called
George. George was an all-rounder on the farm and kept it going
for Peggy for years after Donnie died. He lived in the Bothy through
the kitchen; he had a lovely sense of humour. Peggy always milked
the cows and looked after the hens. George kept the generator going
and raised the calves. He was a shy man and would disappear into
his Bothy after supper.

Norman Burnett

Norman was more of an uncle to the Kirk family. There was nothing
he would not do for them. As a highly qualified electrical engineer
he was very capable indeed.

The most wonderful thing he did was to build a small hydro-electric plant behind Laig Farm. The cliffs were very high; most of the
year there was a respectable head of water tumbling down to the

George Walker,
who looked after
the cows and took
over the running
of the Laig Farm
after Donnie died.

burn below. After heavy rain there was a torrent! Norman brought everything he needed bit by bit from Glasgow and over three or four years completed the scheme. Bill helped him a little and always phoned Norman before leaving England: a) to see if there was anything he could bring; and b) to ask Norman what he wanted Bill to do. Bill was a Consultant Civil Engineer so they complemented each other. When the plant was finally up and running, and when the burn was in full spate, Peggy had too much electricity!

The only alternative form of energy on the island was from two windmills: the large one, which supplied the school; Simon Helliwell created a small one that ran a 40-watt bulb.

Norman Burnett was especially fond of Peggy's children, never having married himself, with an extra-soft spot for Marie. Once he heard that she had a weekend off from school in Fort William, but no way of getting to Eigg, he drove straight down and brought her back. Norman died of cancer in 1996. Marie and Peggy managed to get down to Glasgow to say goodbye to him. He left a large gap in a great many people's lives.

John Cormack and John Chester in the centre.

JOHN CHESTER

'John the Bird' as John Chester is known, is the Scottish Wildlife Warden. He looks after all the S.S.S.I.s on the Island and leads walks every week. You can see so much more when you go with him. He was one of the islanders, along with Marie and Colin Carr, under notice of eviction.

SUSAN BROWNING

No account of our family's love of Eigg would be complete without a brief mention of Sue Browning, the youngest daughter of Jill and Neville Browning of Dormansland, Surrey. There were only six weeks between Rosie and Sue and they grew up almost inseparable. We all loved Sue; she came to Eigg twice with us and loved everything about

Sue Browning in 'bobble' hat; Marie left front, with Jane behind and Rosie on the right.
Angus, aged 10, is driving the tractor in the background.

it. She was enormous fun to be with. I remember her saying, of a
very long walk on one of our expeditions, "My teeth have gone soft!"

Sue persuaded her mother and her friend, Esme, to go to Eigg.
They stayed at Laig. Peter Harcus had brought Father Lennard all
the way on the back of his powerful motorbike and stayed at Laig
at the same time.

Peter Harcus was a pupil in the Oratory School; Father Lennard
was Chaplain to the School and always took one or more of the
boys with him when he went to Eigg.

Sue died of cancer at the age of 21 years. Peter Harcus had gone
to Lourdes that year and came down to Surrey on his bike with some
water from Lourdes for Sue, and a cross that she wore until she
died.

When Sue was dying she had the conviction that if she could get to Iona she would be cured. Cancer is such a cruel, cat and mouse, type of illness. She would have remissions, when she seemed almost well again. During one of these remissions we thought that perhaps if Sue flew to Glasgow and we met her by car we might get her to the Abbey on Iona. The remission did not last and it was obvious Sue would not get there. We decided to go to Iona in her place. We went there from Eigg and stayed one Tuesday night. Was it coincidence, or was it meant to be? – we will never know, but Tuesday is the only day there is a Healing Service in the Abbey. The community there prayed for Sue until she died. Prayers are answered in different ways. Sue had a rare and incurable tumour of the throat; she could have died in distressing and traumatic circumstances with haemorrhaging and choking. Instead she drifted into a peaceful sleep and never knew anything.

A bright star had gone out.

Dr MacLean playing 'Mairi's Wedding' after the wedding of Mairi and Angus.

A TALE OF TWO DOCTORS

Dr MacLean, M.C.

It was most unusual for a holiday to pass without at least one visit to 'the Doctor'. It was a great social event and not to be hurried. You would be greeted by Mrs MacLean, a delightful woman. Adults would be given a cup of tea or coffee and the children orange juice. Then, after much asking after 'so and so' and general catching up with any important gossip, you would eventually get around to the reason for your visit.

If you were too ill to come to him, Dr MacLean would walk over the 'short-cut', kilt swinging, to see you. He had the best car on the island and nothing was going to persuade him to drive it down the mile-long Laig Road – death to any decent car.

The only time Dr MacLean left the Small Isles (if the weather was rough the Lifeboat would take him to the other islands) was during the war. He fought as far as Nijnmagen (in *A Bridge Too Far* battles). He was awarded the Military Cross.

The one thing Dr MacLean would not do was to retire until the NHS had provided a substitute for him. This took a long time but eventually the 'powers that be' gave in and Dr Tiarks and his wife arrived.

Dr Tiarks

It was 1992 – the year my son was to be married in Edinburgh Castle. You can only be married in the tiny Chapel of St Margaret if your Regiment is stationed there, or if your name is Margaret. As you can imagine, nothing was going to stop me going. I woke up a few days before I was due to leave with a very sore throat. I told Peggy I wanted to see the Doctor. Peggy was not at all sure. Dr Tiarks was different – he had an appointment system. I firmly picked up the phone, although I felt a bit nervous about my reception. When I told him the problem I had a terrific welcome. "Yes, do come at 11 a.m." So I duly turned up at 11 a.m. to be met by a film crew and battery of cameras! Would I mind going out and coming up the path again? This I trotted off and did. Inside the surgery were arc lights and the camera man. I was to ignore all this and pretend they were not there.

After a few questions and a good look at my throat he prescribed an antibiotic and off I went, followed by the camera crew.

What had happened was that Dr Tiarks had been an extremely popular doctor in Wales. When he left, Welsh TV had filmed all the farewells and floods of tears, etc. They naturally wanted a record of his arrival on Eigg. My sore throat was perfect. It did not require any undressing and was not embarrassing!

Island life is idyllic in the summer, especially for the tourist, but the long winters are very depressing and, very sadly, Mrs MacLean committed suicide. The islanders were heartbroken; she had been much loved.

Dr MacLean played the pipes. I loved hearing the sound drift across the valley. Fergus Gowans also played the pipes. You could

Dr Tiarks coming off the Sheerwater with his dog.

dance to Fergus' pipes. He went to the Queen's Piper one year for a course on Pibroch.

THE DENTIST

The summer that baby Fiona was born the dentist sailed into Eigg Harbour. Peggy was badly in need of him, so I looked after Fiona and Peggy was rowed out to his boat. She was there most of the day. Goodness knows what he did to her but she was moribund when she came back. I have never seen anyone so ill after a dental visit. Donnie was beside himself with fury and rushed off with murder in his heart. The only thing that saved the dentist from a near-certain death was to 'up anchor' and off before Donnie could get at him!

Peggy did not move for at least three days. Other people's kitchens

Rosie with Fiona before Fiona's wedding at Laig.

Rosie on her own wedding day.

are always more fun, so I enjoyed cooking for 17, and Fiona was such a good baby. She was no trouble and, luckily, bottle fed.

LAWRENCE MCEWAN AND THE COAL

The neighbouring little Isle of Muck was owned by a charming man called Lawrence McEwan. There were never any problems on Muck and the two islands were very close to each other, islanders always going to each other's ceilidhs.

Lawrence was to marry a schoolteacher from a tiny island off Skye. The day of the wedding a Force 8 gale blew up – so Lawrence could not get there.

The following day the wind dropped and there was no reason why the wedding could not go ahead. Then the coal boat arrived! Lawrence said he could not possibly go, the coal was essential!

At this, all his guests and the inhabitants of Muck rose up, metaphorically got him by the scruff of the neck and told him: "Go and get married, we will cope with the coal." So he did. Rosie was

Lawrence McEwan at Angus and Mairi's wedding.

over with all the Eigg guests to the wedding ceilidh. He had chosen well – Jenny was (and still is) a great asset to the island.

Lawrence's brother Ewan built a hotel on Muck. He does all the cooking himself, including fresh bread daily.

The guests soon got used to the handsome chap in a kilt dishing out the porridge in bare feet.

Anne Nimmo Smith (mother of Helen) settled there very happily. She suffers from severe arthritis but is looked after by Lawrence and the other islanders.

THE RADFORDS

The Radfords were the first people we met when we moved into our new house. The day after we moved in, Jane pushed Giles in his pram down our path to welcome us. Giles and Ian were the same age and grew up together; they both went to Brambletye prep school but split up when Ian went to Oundle and Giles to Wellington. They

Pelly and Giles Radford with Angus Kirk,
sitting on the base of the Celtic Cross at Kildonnan.

came together again when they went to Sandhurst and are now
godfathers to each other's children.

Bill and Iain Radford became very good friends, as did Jane and
I. The Radfords had three other children, Toriano, Jo and Pelly,
who had been blind from birth. Iain and Jane were wonderful and
very imaginative with Pelly.

Iain was an officer in the 'Sappers' and, like all army people, moved
every three years or so. It meant that Pelly was continually getting
used to a new house and surroundings: she 'saw' through her hands.

Sunset over Rhum.

I remember her coming to our house one day, feeling a new radiator and saying, "You have got a new radiator like ours." As a teenager, Pelly started to put on some weight. Iain bought a tandem bicycle and put Pelly on the back. It was a great success. Giles had to leave the army. He was deafened in one ear by a faulty intercom in Belfast. There had been a Radford in the army since Wellington's time. Now he has a very successful Prontaprint business in Durham and won the prize for the best Prontaprint in the north-east.

Pelly and Football
I think Pelly enjoyed Eigg – the islanders certainly loved and admired her and still ask about her after all this time. Pelly did not like fur so she did not have a guide dog. That did not stop her from doing anything she wanted to!

She is a great fan of Manchester United. She would go to the matches, following the crowds. Once there, she could listen to the commentary on her Walkman while absorbing the atmosphere.

Pelly married Peter West, also blind from birth, both computer programmers. They were the only blind couple to be married in Westminster Abbey. It was a very beautiful ceremony – I was reduced to tears by the expressions on the faces of the choir looking at Pelly while they were singing. I will never forget the wonderful organ of the Abbey playing Vidor's "Toccata and Fugue" at full strength as we left.

ANGUS MACKINNON

Angus MacKinnon was very important among the crofters on Eigg. He was the senior crofter and, if there is such a thing, the senior member of the Catholic Church on Eigg. Certainly whenever I asked a question about the Church – for instance "how much would it cost to put on a new roof?" – I was told to "ask Angus".

It is not surprising that it was Angus who was designated 'Special Constable'. He had a delightful personality and very strong character. It was his sister, Peggy, who ran the shop when we first went to Eigg and sang Gaelic songs at the ceilidhs when she was alive. Angus handed over the position of Special Constable to Colin Carr when he became ill.

Angus, like so many crofters, always had cows. Years ago he also had Highland cattle. Twice a year the cattle boat comes to collect the cows being sent away to sales on the mainland (one boat is called *Eigg*). All the herd is driven across the island to the pier. Then, somehow, the cows for sale are separated from the rest of the herd – with a great deal of Gaelic! Once that has been accomplished, the bull is let loose. He heads for home – followed by his wives and children.

Angus died in May 2000, after a long fight against cancer. Everyone on Eigg mourned him and I was very sad as I had hoped to see him again in July. Everyone agreed that they would not see his like again.

I was not able to get up to Eigg for the funeral but Peggy Kirk told me that it had been a lovely warm, sunny day – the Hebrides at their very best.

Angus MacKinnon and Mary Bell.

Two hundred people travelled to Eigg for the funeral. Murdoch Grant cancelled his usual timetable and did two runs to get everyone over. It was flat calm. Father Jim Tollhurst from Kent had been staying on Eigg. He had said Mass in Angus' house the day before he died and then stayed on to help the parish priest, Father Donald MacKinnon, with the service. Peggy's sister, Mary Flora from Mallaig, sang a Gaelic hymn as a solo and two pipers – Donald Nicholson from Barra and Ian MacDonald from Uist – played at the graveside. Angus was 73.

In his Homily, Father Donald summed Angus up to perfection when he said:

> *He left us peacefully, gently,*
> *without fuss and without imposition.*
> *We give thanks to God for Angus,*
> *for the man he was.*
> *We give thanks for the man: for his warmth and his humour;*
> *for a welcoming heart;*

for a fine mind;
for all that was fire and independence in him;
for a man of deep natural courtesy;
for a living custodian of the native history and ethos of this Island.
As well as faith, I found in Angus great purity of heart.
"Blessed are the pure of heart: they shall see God."
And I will always hold dear the memory of a man who walked
*   humbly before his God.*
I shall miss his warmth, his welcome and his wisdom,
the easiness of his company,
and the inherent dignity of the man.

The graveyard is by the ruined chapel of Kildonnan. After the burial,
all 200 mourners, with the islanders, went down the hill to Marie
and Colin in Kildonnan Guesthouse. There they were given drinks.
Afterwards they were entertained in the new Tea Room with soup,
sandwiches, cakes, tea and coffee, all made by the islanders. Peggy
made a clouty dumpling and five dozen pancakes.

Angus MacKinnon's highland cattle, about 1970 – sadly no longer on Eigg.

Father Lennard said Mass for Angus in the Brompton Oratory, London, and Father Luke, the Prior, said Mass for him in Worth Abbey, Sussex.

COLIN AND MARIE CARR – AND KILDONNAN

Colin and Marie are extremely valuable to the island so it makes it an even more overwhelming relief that in the end they were not evicted.

Marie is Peggy and Donnie Kirk's eldest daughter. She was an enchanting child and, once she was old enough, amazingly capable. I feel tired just thinking about what she does in a day. Marie is Registrar for the Small Isles, so often has weddings in her house. Apart from bringing up her five delightful children, Donnie, Amy, George, Greg and Francis, she does the school run and cleans the school; runs a superb guesthouse in Kildonnan; makes all her own bread; and, at the drop of a hat, makes 100 rolls for a boat that has just appeared in the harbour! That is just routine. However, the impossible takes a little longer and it would be impossible to list all the other kind things she does on the island. Having been taught to play the accordion by her father, Donnie Kirk, she is often found as part of the band at a Ceilidh.

Colin comes from Stirling and arrived on Eigg as shepherd for Keith Schellenberg. When he married Marie, they made the perfect couple. Colin is incredibly capable and hard-working, a superb shepherd, very kind, an excellent husband and father. Solid to the core and with shining integrity he was the obvious choice to replace Angus MacKinnon as Special Constable. Colin and Marie both would do anything they could for anybody – and frequently do!

When they were first married they lived in Tigh-a-Bhlar in Cleadale, where Donnie was born. Keith then moved them to San-davore Farm where they had more room, and finally to Kildonnan, where Marie could run a guest house.

For some time everything went well. Understandably they needed security and stability which they would only achieve if they had a lease. Keith Schellenberg promised them a lease but it never material-ised and, finally, after not being able to do anything wrong for Keith,

'Young' Duncan Ferguson.

Peggy MacKinnon (centre) with Fergus, right, in the kilt.

Surrey, 1989. Marie and Colin with Donnie, Francis, Greg and George.

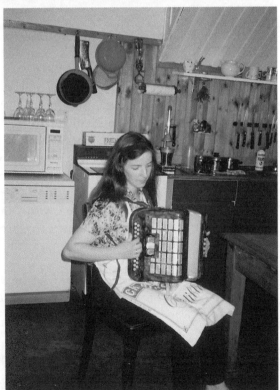

Marie Carr (Peggy Kirk's daughter) playing the accordion at Kildonnan.

they found he had turned against them and they could not do anything right. This ended in an eviction order. Marie was ill with worry. Islanders, especially such valuable islanders as Marie, are priceless. It was unthinkable that she could be evicted, with her family. Rescue came when the Eigg Heritage Trust managed to raise the money to buy Eigg from Maruma, who had purchased the Island from Keith Schellenberg. Colin, Marie and their family now have security and peace of mind – as indeed have all the islanders.

After the death of my husband, when next I was on Eigg, Colin overheard me say that I would have to get a gas fire now I had no one to cut up logs from my wood. It is typical of Colin that he put Marie and his family in his Landrover and drove down to Surrey to cut up wood so I had a supply for the winter!

THE VERY REVEREND FATHER MICHAEL SMITH

Father Michael, although a member of Worth Abbey in Sussex, spent 36 years of his priesthood in Peru. A great deal of his time was spent in the jungle; to get there he would have to travel in an open boat for seven hours on a treacherous river full of rapids.

Father Richard Wilson, the Sub-Prior of Worth Abbey, brought Father Michael to my home in Surrey for tea once when he was on leave. Father Michael noticed a book on Eigg on the table and said, "I have always wanted to go to Eigg." So, with the Abbot's permission, four days later we were on the plane to Inverness, where we collected a hire car for our journey to Arisaig. The following day we crossed over to Eigg and stayed with Marie and Colin Carr in Kildonnan. Fr. Michael got to know the Carrs and Peggy Kirk very well, and also Dolly Ferguson who was still living in Tigh-a-Bhlar then.

Father Michael had previously lost his heart to the Isle of Barra, and having been to Barra with him last year, and met his great friend Father MacQueen, I can see why as it is a very beautiful island indeed. However, he loved Eigg and its people as much, and it was certainly mutual! Father Michael said Mass in the little Catholic Church every day, once he had mastered the lock and got in! The following year we were joined by the Very Revd. Father Luke Jolly,

A recent picture of Angus MacKinnon with Father Michael.

Worth Abbey Prior (half Father Michael's age) who also enjoyed Eigg. They had some good walks together in spite of Father Michael's hip giving him trouble. It was replaced the following year.

We all went again in 2000, this time accompanied by Father Patrick Fludder who was able not only to help with the driving but also to walk with Father Michael as I am not able to walk very far following two knee replacements. Father Patrick is also young – Father Michael is 87 years old in 2000.

13

THREE WEDDINGS ON EIGG

THE WEDDING OF ANGUS KIRK AND MAIRI MACKINNON, 1980

The actual journey to Eigg is always an adventure – sometimes more so than others! The year we went to Eigg for Angus and Mairi's wedding was by far the most eventful. I went ahead with Jane and Rosie, who is a professional London florist and floral decorator; she had been up early to go to Covent Garden to buy all the flowers. Bill went later.

Just getting to Euston was a problem: the siege of the Iranian Embassy was in full flood and central London had been cordoned off. We had to go away from London and swing round to come in

Rosie transporting the flowers for Angus and Mairi's wedding.

on the M40. At Euston we unloaded eight boxes of flowers and five suitcases.

All went well until we reached Rannoch Moor. It must rank as one of the most desolate railways in Britain and furthest from civilisation. We broke down; the guard ran down the line placing detonators on the rails to warn any trains coming up behind to stop. Another chap walked 1½ miles to Rannoch station to 'phone for help. Eventually the train limped into the station and stopped to collect this man. There was a tense moment when the engine would not start again. The rear engine was detached and left at Rannoch. After waiting for the 'down' train to pass, we crept slowly on through Roybridge, Speanbridge and, finally, into Fort William. There the guard helped us move everything from the guard's van into that of the Mallaig train.

Off we went again, past Fass Fern (mentioned in D. K. Bristow's *Flight of the Heron*), home of the Chief of the Camerons, passing Glenfinnan on the superb viaduct with its wonderful view down Loch Shiel. The memorial to Charles Edward Stuart is on the site where he set up his standard and rallied the Clans for the ill-fated '45 Rebellion'. After Glenfinnan there is the joy of the first view of the sea and, if it is clear, the familiar and distinctive outline of Eigg with Rhum towering behind it. On this occasion Peggy had 'phoned before we left home and told us not to go to Glenuig as the Estate boat (the *Ben Morar*) had broken down. Once we reached Arisaig, Rosie rushed to get the flowers from the luggage van and I threw out all our luggage. The Stationmistress, true to West Coast form, knew all about us. She kindly phoned Murdoch Grant who appeared in seconds and whisked us down to the pier where 'Young' Duncan Ferguson was waiting patiently with his brother-in-law, Alec. Carefully we picked our way over rocks and slippery seaweed to their dinghy. Then Duncan steered us with great skill through the shallow, crystal-clear water out to the Eigg ferry. Within yards of the ferry the dinghy's outboard motor spluttered and stopped. We had visions of having to wade out to the dinghy, but Duncan got the outboard going again and everything, including us, was transferred to the Eigg ferry! We had never crossed over to Eigg in such a small craft but we need not have worried – it was one of those days when the sea was a flat calm and looked oily. Our only worry was keeping the flowers cool.

Duncan shared his apple pie with us – it was delicious. He is typical of the West Coast Islanders – quiet, gentle and very kind with impeccable manners.

We arrived at dead low tide. The only way to reach the pier was to climb across the ill-fated *Ben Morar*. Peggy, Angus and Marie Kirk were on the pier to meet us. Angus had to get back to the lambs. Colin arrived with his Landrover at just the right moment. We had had a cup of tea in the Tea Room and bought 'Eigg' t-shirts from the Craft Shop. We stopped to greet Fergus who was sunbathing in his garden and finally arrived at Laig Farm. We wasted no time at all and immediately starting cutting the ends off the flower stalks and putting them into deep water. All sorts of vessels were pressed

Father Hugh Barrett Lennard from Brompton Oratory marrying Angus and Mairi in the Chapel, before its condition deteriorated.

into use once conventional containers ran out. The remaining flowers ended up in the bath!

Father Lennard came in from a long walk and told us there was to be a memorial Mass for Donnie Kirk who had died on that day five years previously (May 1st). This was to be at 6 p.m.

In glorious sunshine Peggy, Fiona and I walked across Laig Bay to the chapel for the service. The island was at its best with wild flowers spilling over every bank. At the church we found most of the islanders and Marie with Donnie and George. After the service we went up to see Granny Kirk and then back along the half-mile of silver sand for our evening meal.

After 'buttering' 12 loaves, Rosie and I set off in the van to take the flowers to the church – at least we would have done if it had started! It still would not start after running it backwards, downhill. Angus, George – and the dogs – helped us move all the flowers into Angus' Landrover. So, after more dramas than we usually encounter on our journeys to Eigg, the flowers finally reached their destination after their long journey from Covent Garden.

It was so peaceful in the chapel, with only the sound of the larks and the sea outside. Rosie did not get her talent for floristry and flower arranging from me. However I am a useful assistant, handing flowers up and clearing up afterwards. Peter Harcus brought us a wonderful tray of tea, home-made scones, jam and cheese. We had worked for four hours without stopping, so it was very welcome.

Peter Harcus and Father Lennard were concerned about space in the chapel. The seating was easy to count but we all joined in standing against the wall so they could count how many people could stand. We took photos of the transformed chapel before walking back along the shore, paddling in the sea to cool our hot feet. After yet another cup of tea we set off with Peggy to the hall. On the way we stopped for a drink with Fergus and Leslie Gowans, and to pick up the nice salad Leslie had made for the reception.

Natalie arrived to help and together we raided the Lodge garden, and then decorated the hall with bamboo and cherry blossom. At that point, Mairi's mother arrived from Glasgow, feeling left out of things. We all made the sandwiches and coleslaw and arranged the stage, then we left for Laig Farm with a fuming Peggy who felt she

had done everything. Father Lennard made peace and we all went
to bed early.

The day of the wedding

As soon as we had finished breakfast, Rosie started wiring the flowers
and leaves for Mairi's bouquet, bridesmaids' head-dresses and baskets. The two mothers, Peggy and Ann, had sprays and all the men
involved had 'buttonholes'. I helped wire the flowers and leaves but
was painfully slow. Rosie, apart from being a gifted florist trained
at Constance Spry, worked with exceptional speed. (Because of this,
she had been chosen to decorate St Martins-in-the-Field for the
Memorial Service for Airey Neave, M.P., who was murdered by the
I.R.A. – the Security authorities only allowed one hour). Peggy and
her Dutch friend, Gretchi, kept us going with endless cups of tea.
Towards the end we were working against the clock.

Rosie made the bridesmaids' baskets first, then assembled Mairi's
bouquet, sprays for the two mothers and seven white carnation
buttonholes for the groom, best man and ushers. We worked so hard
that we had not even looked up when Bill, Jane and Peggy's family
from Uist came into the kitchen. Rosie took the flowers over to
Mairi about 3.30. Bill, Jane, Rosie and I left at 3.55 – wedding at 4
p.m.!

It was a wonderful sight at the Church – the many kilts provided
lots of colour. Lawrence McEwan looked especially picturesque and
became the subject of many photographs. The guests had arrived in
every type of transport, including tractors and trailers! Finally the
bride arrived in the one 'good' car on the Island, belonging to
Dr MacLean, bedecked with white ribbons.

Mairi looked lovely. Her father escorted her in, piped into the
church by Peggy's nephew, then she and Angus sat at one side of
the altar. Father Lennard conducted the service beautifully and read
out a telegram with a Papal Blessing for the couple. Father Lennard's
homilies were apt to 'go on a bit': as legally they had to be married
before 5 p.m. or their marriage would not be valid, Peter put a clock
on the altar. After the marriage service there was a Nuptial Mass.
Dougie MacKinnon fired a salute! Dr MacLean played "Amazing
Grace" on the pipes during communion, then – what else but "Mairi's

Wedding" as they came out into the warm evening sunshine. I had left the south in freezing, miserable weather, but did not even need a cardigan over my silk dress.

After many photographs we all climbed into the various vehicles to go to the Hall for the reception. The whole of Eigg, except Sara Campbell who was disabled, came, plus a large party from the Isle of Muck and a coachload of 50 from Glasgow. Somehow the 220 guests were transferred to the hall. Here they were all given whisky for the toasts, then cut the cake and read the telegrams – one of them from my son, Ian Orr. There was plenty to eat for everyone – cold meats, turkey and lots of different kinds of salads, desserts and, of course, the cake.

It is so sensible in the islands; no one expects the bride's mother – or in this case the bridegroom's mother as Mairi's parents lived in Glasgow – to provide all the food. Everyone contributes one kind of dish or another.

After a while, Mairi went to change into a dress she could dance in and the Ceilidh started. They had hired the best band in the Hebrides. The accordionist, Ian MacLachlan, was brilliant and played very fast. He has made many records and tapes. We enjoyed the Highland dances as well as one or two 'modern' dances. Rhoddie and Lachie grumbled about the modern ones! Pat Macnab, who had been born in Laig Farm, came with his wife and thoroughly enjoyed the evening. Norman took me, with Bill, Jane and Rosie, back to Laig Farm at 3.30 a.m. It had been a wonderful day and the party was by no means over. Peggy MacKinnon and her sister sang Gaelic songs – one was a 'spinning' song; Willy Shields and Anne MacKinnon sang "My Way". The 'official' piper played 'Pibroch' music in the interval when an enormous tea was provided. Some of the guests did not go to bed at all and just went straight to church next morning!

The next day, Sunday, everyone woke up late. Then, after breakfast, there was great consternation at Laig when George, who had done a little too well with the whisky, was still 'out cold'. We realised that someone else would have to milk the cows. We had a great deal of advice from the Uist farmers and Pat McNab – but not much help! Finally, we dug George out of bed and he roused sufficiently to milk a few of the cows. Then he fell heavily in the byre and hurt his back so, with great difficulty, we got him back to bed.

Amazingly, Peter Harcus – a Londoner – came up trumps! The cows liked him and he milked them twice a day until he left, by which time George was back on his feet.

It was another glorious day. A football match developed on the beach with Angus joining in – with no sign of his bride! Later, everyone crowded into Laig Farm kitchen. Eventually Peggy escaped and went down to the caravan where Peggy's sisters were staying.

We had a delightful picnic in the garden with Jean and Alastair White, a couple from Glasgow who had been coming to Eigg for as long as we had.

All day Landrovers had been charging up and down, collecting wood for a giant bonfire. All ages gathered round it with Ian, the accordionist, playing. We danced on the sand by moonlight, and sang. It was a beautiful, clear night, with the stars appearing more brilliant than they do in the south. It was lovely to see everyone's faces in the firelight. We walked back to Laig across the sand about 1.30 a.m. – the end of a wonderful wedding.

The following day, Monday, Jane and Rosie were up early as this was their last day. We all went down to the pier about 11.30 a.m. and bought some more things in the Craft Shop. Gradually all the guests from Glasgow and all the islanders arrived bit by bit.

The *Sheerwater* had arrived by then. It was supposed to leave at 2 p.m., but when Angus and Mairi arrived, Angus remembered he had left his Birth Certificate behind. He needed this to get his passport. We were afraid the boat would leave without them. In the end, although Angus was back in time, poor Noel – Peggy's brother-in-law – delayed the boat. He had an acute attack of pain from a kidney stone; the Doctor ran down the road to give him some Pethidine. While everyone was waiting, Ian was still playing his accordion and another Ceilidh broke out with everyone dancing on the pier.

Finally they all got on the boat and came to the side to wave goodbye, with another piper playing on board. The boat listed heavily, but it is a very safe, stable boat and disaster was avoided. The other side, when they arrived at Arisaig, it took ages to ferry

Guests from Angus Kirk's wedding leaving on the *Sheerwater*.

them ashore by dinghy. Norman took Jane and Rosie to Glasgow by car, where they stayed the night with Jean and Alastair White and their daughter, Louise. The following day they crossed over to Edinburgh and were able to take their grandmother out to lunch before getting the London train.

The wedding guests were very late getting back to Glasgow; the brakes of the coach had jammed!

Next day (Tuesday), we had used all the petrol in the van, so Colin very kindly lent us his Landrover. Bill and I went back to the church and Marie helped me take down all the flowers. She took one arrangement and we put the rest in the Landrover. We went first to Marion Carr, and gave her some of the flowers, as she had baked so many cakes for the wedding. Then down to Kildonnan to put flowers on Donnie's grave. We did not know which was Donnie

Kirk's grave but noticed the bridesmaids had placed their flowers on the MacKinnons' grave. I ran down the hill to Mary Campbell to ask her to show us and found Leslie Gowans there. Leslie came up with us and showed us the grave – next to the ruined Chapel.

We noticed the ancient statue of the Madonna was missing from its niche in the Chapel wall. This had been taken into safe keeping by Angus MacKinnon and is still there.

I took the rest of the flowers back to Laig Farm, except for one arrangement which Bill, Catriona Anderson (who later married Ronnie Dyer, the skipper of the *Sheerwater*) and I took to Sara Campbell who had been unable to get to the wedding. On the way back we stopped to watch Simon Helliwell and his family building their new house. They were just filling the footings with concrete. We called in to young Duncan Ferguson who very reluctantly agreed to let us pay him for bringing us over in his boat.

We stopped for a coffee with Marie. She and Colin were living in Tigh-a-Bhlar. After lunch, Dr MacLean walked over the hills to look at George's back (Dr MacLean would never risk bringing his car down the dreadful 'Laig Road'). It was a good week before George was able to walk again.

After lunch I finally had time to take slides of flowers for my talk on Eigg. I was lucky and found marsh marigolds reflected in the water and carpets of primroses; many varieties of orchids; yellow flags (wild Iris); sundew plants and the more attractive 'flycatcher' plant, Butterwort, as well as wild hyacinths. In England they would be called bluebells. The Scottish name is more accurate – the bluebell of Scotland is the harebell.

Up early the following day we sadly set off from Laig with Father Lennard who was returning to Brompton Oratory. We waited until the last minute to climb out of the Eigg Ferry and up the ladder to the Skye Ferry (the *Pioneer*) to go back to Mallaig. The fantastic Highland wedding had come to an end at last.

Colin, Peggy, Marie and Fiona have come south for my daughters' weddings which must have seemed very tame in comparison to an island wedding.

FIONA KIRK AND MARK CHERRY, 1989

Fiona Kirk and Mark Cherry were married in the spring of 1989. Bill and I were booked into the Old Library Guest House and Restaurant at Arisaig and we had planned to go on to Ardnamurchan after the wedding. As it turned out we did not go. Bill was taken gravely ill. This meant that Jane and Rosie went by themselves, taking all the flowers for Fiona and the wedding cake I had made and decorated from a picture Fiona had cut out of a magazine. I enjoyed cakecraft and had been fortunate in my tutor, Stanley Levy – a gifted craftsman and excellent tutor.

Jane and Rosie had an eventful journey. First the train broke down on Ranmore, the bleakest and most inaccessible place to break down.

The train only broke down on Rannoch Moor twice – but both

Angus, Marie, Alastair and 'D.J.' Kirk after Fiona's wedding to Mark Cherry.

times we were on our way to a wedding on Eigg. It was almost a repeat performance, even to the crossing.

The driver had run back 3 miles to the last station and then he put detonators on the line to alert any trains coming on from the rear. Another engine was despatched from Fort William but, of course, by the time they reached Fort William the Mallaig train had long since gone. British Rail put all the passengers from the train onto minibuses. Every time the bus went round a corner, all the boxes of flowers and the 3 boxes with tiers of wedding cake slid from one end of the bus to the other – then back again. All the passengers gasped every time it happened, knowing what was inside! When they arrived at Arisaig they found the *Sheerwater* ferry was not running and a very small boat was sent to collect them. It could have been a very 'hairy' crossing but was actually a flat calm. In fact, Rosie told me afterwards that her only problem had been keeping the flowers cool as it was a very hot day. The wedding sounded lovely. Rosie and Fiona had grown up together and it gave Rosie much pleasure to be able to do Fiona's flowers for her, and decorate the Church.

ROSIE ORR AND RICK ROBERTS, 1994

Both Rosie and Rick had been let down by their first partners and the regimental friends of Rosie's first husband closed ranks round her and were very supportive, in particular one Hugh Stafford-Smith and his wife, Lizzy. It happened that Hugh also knew Rick. When the time came for the regimental ball, Hugh said to Rosie, "Why don't you come with us, it will do you good." Rosie replied that she did not feel like going – especially without a partner. Off went Hugh to Rick – "Rick, Rosie is feeling very low, it would be very kind if you took her to the ball." Until then, Rick had given the same reply as Rosie. Hugh then went back to Rosie – "Rosie, Rick is feeling very low" etc. It worked! Rick took Rosie to the ball and they never looked back. The Colonel danced with Rosie early in the evening and told her how good it was to see her there.

Rosie had taken Rick to Eigg and he had instantly fallen in love with the island. They both decided that Eigg was the only place for

An island wedding feast prepared by Marie and Lillian at Kildonnan for Rosie and Rick.

the wedding. Luckily for them, Marie Kirk was Registrar for the Small Isles. It was lucky again that Marie and Rosie had grown up together. Rick stayed at Kildonnan and Rosie at Laig Farm because she regarded Laig as her second home. The Bothy was bursting with flowers and had never smelled so good! Rosie's friend, Gilla Bruce, a gifted Knightsbridge florist, came up with her ex-naval husband Gordon, and did all Rosie's flowers. The generator played up and Gordon got it going again with knowledge from his naval days.

The reception was at Kildonnan and Marie was responsible for the super food, helped by Lillian, Dr Tiarks' wife. Keith Schellenberg donned a chauffeur's cap and pretended to be a chauffeur, driving Rosie to her wedding in his Rolls Royce, the car that had a sad end.

It was the first time that Bill's brother Ian (Mhor) and his wife

Rosie on her wedding
day in Keith
Schellenberg's Rolls
Royce; he pretended to
be a chauffeur.

Rosie Orr after her
marriage to Rick Roberts
in 1994.

Joan (known to the family as Wiz) and some of their children had been to Eigg. It was lovely to have them there, as well as Rick's parents, Michael and Valerie Roberts, and two of Rick's brothers. Close friends came from the island and we all squeezed into the kitchen where Rosie and Rick had insisted that Marie should marry them. It was the largest room in Kildonnan, so it made sense. It was difficult for Marie to marry someone she knew so well but she conducted the service superbly. She explained the difference between Scottish and English law and somehow, in her own way, made the whole ceremony dignified and very special.

While there was not room for the whole island to come to the wedding, there was plenty of room for everyone for the Ceilidh in the evening.

Rosie and Rick have been back every year for their anniversary and, once the children Claudia and Tamsin arrived, they went as well!

Rosie told me that the morning of the wedding, she and Fiona were going somewhere in Fiona's Landrover, when they saw Rick in the distance. It is unlucky for the bride to be seen by the bridegroom before the wedding, so they hid in the cottage of John Chester, the Scottish Wildlife Warden.

14

PIPPO

WE HAD Siamese cats from the first year of our marriage. My aunt bought a very smart lady. She had two kittens and my aunt gave them both to us – a girl and a boy. My brother-in-law had a friend, Eirian, who was married to John Wain, novelist and professor of poetry at Oxford, and I made the mistake of asking her advice on names. Without drawing breath she said firmly: "Tamburlaine and Zenocrates!" I was stunned but the die was cast. They rapidly became Tammy and Zinny. Tammy was a wool-eater. This was very embarrassing. Twinsets were in fashion and visiting friends would get warm and take off their cardigans. When they were leaving they would pick up the cardigans to find half the backs were missing. All my relations stopped knitting for the children – they saw no reason why they should feed my cat! Zinny thought he was very clever but was not sure what to do. I remember one occasion when he was being told off for eating one of Ian's bootees; Zinny sat listening to all this, then trotted off and came back with the other. She reckoned he might as well be killed for a sheep as for a lamb.

In due course, when we had moved to the country, Zinny had her own kittens. Peggy Kirk said she would love to have one. We set off with kitten in a basket, plus Jane, Rosie and Sue Browning, by motor rail. Kitten did not like this. He howled (as only Siamese can) all the way. I let him out of his basket and he stood on my chest and howled. It is a long way to Fort William and we did not have a wink of sleep. Finally, when we carried him along the mile long road to Laig, he dropped off, exhausted.

Father Lennard was staying at Laig. He asked the kitten's date of birth. "Ah," said Father Lennard, "that is St Phillip's Day," so he became Pippo.

Pippo loved Eigg – so much freedom and exciting things to play with. He became Alastair's cat, but Donnie liked him also and he

Rock pools at the end of Laig Bay, with Rhum in the distance.

was the only cat allowed in the kitchen. Pippo had a wonderful life on Eigg, but sadly a short one. He was the same colour as a rabbit and the eagle took him.

15

WELCOME ADDITIONS TO THE EIGG POPULATION

S EVERAL NON-ISLANDERS have come to Eigg and stayed, contributing much in their own ways.

Simon and Karen Helliwell had already arrived. Simon is a gifted carpenter; he and his wife decided to take their family away from the 'rat race' and valued Eigg's quality of life. Simon's skills as a carpenter – and much more – have proved a 'godsend' to the island. Karen proved to be a superb secretary when the time came for the islanders to raise the money to buy Eigg and manage it afterwards.

Natalie Yardey, a gifted jeweller and silversmith, arrived and married John who is postman and ferryman. Natalie developed cancer, which thankfully has not reappeared but she left John to be nearer medical help. Their two delightful sons divide their holidays between parents.

Camille Dressler, who is French, has lived happily on Eigg for 17 years. She published a remarkable history of Eigg in 1998. Her painstaking research was mind-boggling. Her book starts around 6,000 BC and is a book not to be missed. Anyone reading her book will learn much, not only of Eigg, but of Scottish history as well.

Theresa is an artist who has produced some lovely paintings and keeps the Craft Shop going with her cards and paintings. I feel her own signature is an oystercatcher – there is usually one in everything she paints.

Joy and Barry Williams bought the house opposite the shop. They are a delightful and very kind English couple who have retired to Eigg very happily. They are both gifted and talented gardeners, as their garden will demonstrate!

Maggie and Wess Fyffe and their children have proved a great joy to the Island. Wess (an Irishman) works their croft more thoroughly than any of the other crofters. Maggie and Wess produced very nice crafts during the winter – some charming woven rugs and wonderful knitted wool boots. These were welcomed by all ages, but the little ones for toddlers starting to walk were invaluable. The suede soles were supple for tiny feet – and they stayed on!

Once the battle for the Island commenced, Maggie left her crafts and became the spokeswoman. She was heard on radio and seen on television (the Islanders were too shy). Then, when their generator was working – she went out on the Internet to Scots all over the world.

Maggie and Wess were, and still are, musicians and an essential part of the Ceilidh band.

Maggie is very warm-hearted and you are always sure of a kindly welcome and coffee – as long as you do not call too early!

Maggie and Wess Fyffe's Crafts.

16

FORMER OWNERS OF EIGG

THE RUNCIMANS (VISCOUNT WALTER RUNCIMAN AND SIR STEPHEN RUNCIMAN, HIS YOUNGER BROTHER)

When we visited Eigg for the first time, Eigg was still owned by Lord Runciman. This was the golden age with the perfect owner. For one thing, Lord Runciman and his historian brother, Sir Stephen Runciman, did not expect to get anything back from the island. Lord Runciman looked after the islanders as if they were his own family. He gave them free coal; their houses were repaired; machinery arrived and was maintained; the land and animals were looked after. There was full employment, which was not the case in any other period before or after when the island was under one owner.

Sir Stephen loved the peace he found on Eigg for his writing. I saw him once, standing on a mound near Kildonnan, looking towards the mainland. He designed the Lodge gardens on the lines of Inverewe and Tresco in the Scillies.

I give a slide talk on Eigg, and in about 1995 I went to a village in Kent. On only four occasions have I found anyone in the audience who has been to Eigg. On this occasion I found two – a charming old lady called Kirsty Guthrie, and her daughter Caroline Gould who drew the lovely line illustration of Garmisdale. They had brought their photo album.

As a family, they had spent two summers on the island, staying in Garmisdale, to avoid the blitz in south-east England. Kirsty was Sir Stephen's cousin and she phoned me to tell me about Sir Stephen's birthday party, with 400 guests, including Princess Margaret.

I went to visit Kirsty twice and we phoned each other frequently; she was deeply interested in the politics of the island. I always phoned her when I returned from Eigg or had any news. I was deeply saddened by her death at the age of 94 in 1999 and miss her very much.

MR EVANS

Mr Evans bought the island from the Runcimans. He was a Welsh farmer and tried to use the same farming methods he used in Wales. This was a mistake. He also stayed in Wales and did not live on Eigg, so he sold the island.

COMMANDER RICHARD FARNHAM SMITH

Mr Evans sold Eigg to Commander Richard Farnham Smith, from Sussex. The first thing that Fergus Gowans did was to look him up in the Navy List: he was not there! Later he confessed to Fergus that he was a 'Commander' in the Fire Service.

Mr Smith promised to revitalise the island by opening a school for handicapped boys. The school was supposed to bring in teachers and other workers, with leisure facilities and light industries. This was to be done through the Anglyn Trust, described as a non-profit-making Christian charity, founder and principal – Farnham Smith! The only sign of the Trust was a flag flown from the roof of the Lodge.

The first thing he did was to fill the Ceilidh Hall with bags of cement and lock it – so the whole time that he was owner of Eigg there were no ceilidhs. The islanders never went back to pure country dancing and singing Gaelic songs when the hall opened again under Keith Schellenberg. There are still a lot of Scottish Reels but modern dancing plays a large part now.

In 1974 The *Mail on Sunday* discovered that Farnham Smith was 'slave-driving' the £250.00 a term boys. Only a handful ever arrived and they were 'spirited' off the island before some police arrived – and the school had no plans for any more.

Farnham Smith nearly sank Donnie Kirk's boat, the *St Donan*. Smith had bought a 140-ton schooner and anchored it off the pier. The water there is unsuitable for ships exceeding 70 tons (which is why the Caledonian MacBrayne Ferry cannot come into the pier). During a storm the schooner broke adrift and rammed Donnie Kirk's boat. It took three months to repair and cost Donnie £1,200: Farnham Smith refused to pay.

He threatened to ban all transport and make the islanders pay to use an 'Egg-shaped' bus. However, he found he could not interfere with transport on a public highway. He paid rock-bottom wages to farmhands and withdrew the perks of free coal and potatoes; he drove at least two families off the island and lured others to non-existent jobs.

Fergus Gowans was the County Councillor for the Small Isles. He was horrified at what was happening to Eigg and did some research into the Anglyn Trust. Farnham Smith did not like this and attacked Fergus on the pier. Fergus had to have stitches for a cut in his head and treatment for bruises.

Farnham Smith wanted to cut all the trees down and sell the wood to Ireland. Fortunately that did not happen, as Eigg's trees are one of its beauties. Sir Andrew Gilchrist, Chairman of the Highlands & Islands Development Board, travelled over by boat to discuss Eigg's future with Farnham Smith. When he heard Sir Andrew was coming Farnham Smith hurriedly left Eigg.

Dr MacLean said the previous owners were gentlemen. When the islanders had had as much as they could take, they stuck a letter on the shop noticeboard telling Farnham Smith to leave. As he was finally leaving, Dr MacLean swung a claymore round his head and cried out, "If you come back I will cut your head off!"

When Mr Evans, the previous owner, heard what had been happening he was very upset and said he would never have sold the island to Farnham Smith if he had known what the latter would do.

KEITH SCHELLENBERG

Keith Schellenberg is the only owner of Eigg whom we have known personally. He and his wife (known at that time as Lady Margaret, and very wealthy!) bought the island between them. This was to cause problems later when they came to divorce.

Keith was capable of great kindness: one of the first things he did was to fly Donnie Kirk back to Eigg in his private plane from the Glasgow hospital. Donnie was then able to die at home, surrounded by his family and friends and within sight and sound of the sea – instead of in a hospital ward hundreds of miles away. Keith also flew Fergus to hospital once in the helicopter when Leslie was away.

He was an amazing character with boundless energy. A keen bobsleigher, he also took part in the 'Round Britain' power boat race.

He loved Eigg and genuinely wanted to do the best for the island. He was a teetotaller and vegetarian and banned blood sports on the island (including fishing). It *might* have worked if he could have brought himself to give the islanders the leases they needed to have to enable them to get grants to repair their houses.

Keith and Bill, and Bill's brother Ian (Mhor), were at Oundle together, in the same House. Keith and Ian were the same age, born in 1930. Most of the time Keith called Bill 'Ian'. We were invited to dinner at the Lodge – first when he was married to Lady Margaret and then later when he was married to Suki (General Urquhart's daughter). On that occasion Keith had found a group of bedraggled, highly intellectual French people soaked to the skin and had invited them as well. I suspect both wives and cooks were long-suffering and used to rising to challenges. It was a delightful evening. The French were a mixture of politicians, authors, etc. Rosie exchanged with one of their daughters. Bill and I were invited to stay in their summer chateau when we delivered Rosie. There were so many people staying they had two sittings for dinner!

Sadly, over the years, relations between Keith and the islanders went from bad to worse. Every building on the island, including the Lodge, needed urgent repairs. Keith was under a lot of pressure. His marriage to Suki was coming to an end and Lady Margaret (now remarried, she was Mrs Williams) complained that she was not getting a return for the money she had put in to buy Eigg. She took Keith to court and won. This meant that Keith had to sell Eigg to repay her.

About that time, Keith's Rolls Royce (in which, having donned a chauffeur's cap, he had kindly driven Rosie from Eigg to Kildonnan for her wedding) burnt down in its shed. Keith was convinced that this was the work of one or more of the islanders. It is impossible to keep a secret on an island. No one on Eigg was responsible. Flares were kept in the shed; they must have self-ignited.

Keith started issuing eviction notices to islanders whose families had lived there for generations. For some reason he would not agree to Council houses being built on Cleadale. John Chester, known locally as 'John the Bird', the Scottish Wildlife Warden, was also issued with an eviction notice.

The last time I saw Keith was in the 'Old Library' Restaurant in Arisaig. I was having dinner with Father Wynn and Father Michael (a Benedictine monk from Worth Abbey). Keith came in with his friend, Clanranald, and joined us for dinner.

'MARUMA'

Keith sold Eigg to a strange German 'artist' who called himself Maruma. His idea of art was to burn a canvas on one side – whatever appeared on the other side was his so-called 'Art'. These he sold for four figures! He *said* he was a millionaire and was going to put seven million pounds into the island. The only thing he actually did was to start a survey into extending the Pier. This apparently required scaffolding. All the children thought this 'climbing frame' was for them!

I am not even sure if Maruma did own Eigg. He started to clear all the scrap metal from tractors and cars which had 'died'. It transpired he had put Eigg up against a loan to a man in Hong Kong.

These were people's lives being bargained with. The islanders had had enough. I was so proud of them. They embarked on raising two million pounds to buy Eigg. They had two concerts in Glasgow and all the usual appeals, raffles, etc. When the generator was working Maggie Fyffe went out on the Internet to Scots and friends of Eigg all over the world. TV, radio and newspapers carried the story. After some nail-biting hitches they had done it. Eigg belonged to them.

On 12th June 1997 a plaque was unveiled next to the Clachna Daoine (the stone of the people) by Dougie MacKinnon (who had driven us around Eigg on our first visit, with Fergus) and Dolly Ferguson, the two oldest islanders. A new, golden dawn was breaking.

The following year I landed on the Pier and could not believe my eyes. In one year they had built a superb building. This housed the new Tea Room; the new shop, large and well stocked, replacing the old corrugated iron hut, which had no electricity or running water (the new shop had a freezer, a refrigerated cabinet and even a refrigerated counter); and the Post Office. (The Tea Room deserves a better name – we had an elegant candlelit dinner there as guests of Joy and Barry, an English couple who had settled very happily on Eigg). In the centre of the building are three 'loos' (one fully equipped for the disabled), and Fergus' sofa – while it lasts. Finally, at the end, there is the new Craft Shop. All three are serviced by one generator.

The islanders had appointed a project manager and feasibility studies were considering, amongst other things, the future of the Lodge.

The atmosphere on Eigg was wonderful. After all the strain and heartache of the previous years they could all relax and be in control of their own lives.

On my way back to the *Sheerwater*, when I was leaving, I suddenly saw a large new house where for years there had been a shell. "What's that?" I asked. "Oh," said Colin casually, "that is the new centre for wildlife studies!" Now they can all plan the rest of their lives in safety. The only worries are the prices Colin can get for his sheep!

17

BILL

WILLIAM TANNAHILL ORR was born in 1928 on the Isle of Wight. The name 'Tannahill' was taken from that of a relation – the poet who wrote "Ye Banks and Braes of Bonnie Scotland" among other things. Bill was the middle son of three between Alex, the eldest and Ian (Mhor) the youngest and was the only one not born in India. He and his brother Ian came back to England to school at five years of age. They went to a farm for their holidays – after prep school in East Anglia.

They went to Oundle School in St Anthony House. Bill went from there to Cambridge to read Engineering; he joined the Cambridge Air Squadron and got his pilot's licence. On one occasion he flew up to Edinburgh to see his parents who, by that time, had returned to a large flat on two floors in Learmonth Terrace, just over the Dean Bridge. Bill's first job as a qualified civil engineer was with a group of civil engineers building a hydro-electric scheme on Loch Quoich on the west coast of Scotland. Until then, although he was a pure Scot, he had never been north of Edinburgh. Bill fell in love with the West Coast and the Highlands so it was no surprise that he loved Eigg so much. All the engineers and their wives lived in caravans; for a change and relaxation they were frequent visitors to the Spean Bridge Hotel. They thought nothing of driving to Inverness for a haircut!

Working and living so close to one another forged lifelong friendships – Henry and Moira Roulston, Meg and David Nesbit, Alec and Betty Gilbertson. After Quoich, Bill came south to London and joined R. T. James and Partners. There he made friends for life with Tony Lambert and Geoff Smith, also Civil Engineers. Geoff Smith became an expert in soil mechanics and lectured on the subject at the University in Edinburgh, where they lived.

Geoff was responsible for the soil mechanics of the Forth Road Bridge, Edinburgh. Before the road was completed, Geoff took Bill

Bill and Ian.

to walk over on the 'cat walk'! Geoff also produced the only textbook
on soil mechanics and is now a PhD.

By the time Bill was a partner in the consulting firm of R. T.
James and Partners, he valued the opportunity he got on Eigg to
totally 'switch off' from all his responsibilities. He and Donnie Kirk
became very close friends. Donnie bought Peggy down to stay with
us and we had a lovely time showing them around the south.

In 1989 Bill was about to retire and thought it would be a good
idea to take up golf. Tony Lambert, his closest friend – who had
been his best man – lent him some clubs and off Bill went for his
first lesson. I heard his car return but Bill did not come into the
house. I went to see what he was doing and was shocked to find
him in great pain, not able to get out of the car. I telephoned the
surgery and Dr Tim Taylor came: it took both of us an hour to get
Bill out of the car and upstairs to bed.

Bill had arrived at the golf course and went to swing his clubs on
his back which went into spasm. The Instructor managed to help
him back into the car and he drove home. We were lucky to know
one of, if not the, best physiotherapist in the south of England, Gill
New. Gill came to treat Bill and he was improving. One Monday
when Gill came to treat him I told her Bill's back had gone into
spasm again. Gill said: "It should not have done that." Later she
told me that she had received a 'warning flash'. Bill improved again
and was even thinking of going back to work. He had gone to wash
in the bathroom when I heard him call. He said, "My back has 'gone'
again, you will have to help me back to bed." Half an hour after
that Bill called. To my horror he said, "I can't feel my legs!"

Bill died three weeks later in the Surrey Marsden Hospital from
advanced cancer of the spine. He was paralysed from the chest down.
This did help a little for all the family to come to terms with it. He
was such an active man it would have been a living death had he
lingered. What was amazing was that he had had so little warning.

Tony Lambert said of Bill, in his address at the Memorial Service:
"Bill always did everything just a little better than anyone else."

Bill died on 19th May 1989 and I took his ashes to Eigg. Father
Lennard was staying at the time and he placed the ashes in the
Church overnight. The next day, Colin Carr had dug a little grave

between those of Fergus Gowans and Neil the Shepherd, and Father Lennard gave a short service. Peggy Kirk, with her daughters Marie Carr and Fiona came, as did Angus MacKinnon and Keith Schellenberg. Marie had prepared a lovely tea for everyone afterwards. Sandy Buchanan, a friend of ours who lived near us in the south, had made a temporary cross from some of the local trees that had come down in the hurricane, yet I wanted a permanent stone.

I had started N.A.D.F.A.S. Church Recording by then. Three months before Bill died we had a speaker, Richard Grasby, who was a stone-cutter. He is a delightful man and one of the best stone-cutters in the country. I was talking about a stone for Bill to some other Church Recorders and said: "I should love Richard Grasby to do Bill's stone." They said: "Why don't you ask him for a quote," which I did. Richard's quote was only slightly more than another one I had received so I asked him to do Bill's stone. He was wonderful. He chose granite, that would survive all the west coast weather. At the lecture he had given he had begged us to put something about the person on memorial stones – more than name and date. He was very helpful with suggestions about the wording. The stone read:

William Tannahill Orr

1928–1989

A loving Husband, Father and Grandfather

A Scot who loved Eigg and its people

A brilliant Civil Engineer who restored Ely Cathedral

The last line was a slight exaggeration as Bill had restored one of the towers of Ely Cathedral. At the time I was not in a fit state to notice that.

The following year, once the stone was ready, Richard told me he wanted to set it himself. He was bringing his wife Juliet up from Grantchester, where they lived.

The stone had been delivered to my house. Jane had 'swopped' cars with me as her estate car had no ledge to lift the stone over. There was a dreadful performance in loading the stone in the south – it took seven men, with dire warnings that we would need a crane at the other end.

Jane and her three-year old Lucy came with me. I booked us into

One of the towers of Ely Cathedral, restored by William Orr.
Original line and wash illustration by John Rees-Davies.

The Old Library Guest House and Restaurant; also Richard and Juliet who were coming the following day. We all stayed with Marie at Kildonnan.

I had chartered the *Sheerwater* and Murdoch Grant, the owner, told me they had to load it at dead high tide, 7 a.m., so the *Sheerwater* was level with the dock. I had murmured about a crane, but when we backed the car up to the boat, Murdock and Ronnie, the skipper, picked up the stone and walked onto the boat without turning a hair! When we arrived at Eigg our friends were waiting to greet us and I was so busy hugging everyone I momentarily forgot about the stone. I asked Peggy where it was. "Oh," she said, "Colin has put it in the Landrover!" I rather wished the seven chaps from the south had been there.

The following day Richard came off the *Sheerwater* carrying his little bucket of cement. Colin had taken for granted that he would do the digging. Richard would have none of it: he insisted on doing everything himself. In the afternoon Father Jim, a friend of Peggy Kirk's, very kindly offered to bless the stone. Richard and Juliet said it was the very first time that they had attended a blessing at any of Richard's stones. Lucy played 'peek-a-boo' from behind the stone, which brought a lump to my throat and Jane's. Once more Marie Carr produced a fantastic tea, bless her.

It was a privilege and delight to have Richard and Janet on Eigg for the weekend. We took them to the Singing Sands and I have a movie of Richard dancing on the sands. We went in search of seals in the dark and laughed a great deal. They were captivated by the island and its people, and we were captivated by them.

18

FLOWERS, BIRDS AND FOSSILS

EIGG IS A PARADISE for anyone who loves flowers and birds, whether like me you just enjoy them but cannot remember half the names, or whether you are a serious botanist and/or ornithologist. There are seven S.S.S.I.s on the island. John Chester was appointed Scottish Wildlife Warden by Keith Schellenberg (and was very nearly evicted by him). He has done a wonderful job managing the island's wild life and plants. He has published a list of all the plants found on Eigg – some very rare – and a superb book with excellent photographs of the birds of Eigg. Both can be obtained from the Craft Shop. John leads a walk every week for anyone interested in the plants and birds – well worth joining him; you can learn a great deal.

I was 'pottering' near Laig one day and came across some fossils.

Nest of Ringed Plover, with eggs.

A Cormorant fishing.

Even my untutored eye could tell they had been oysters. Some friends living near me in Sussex are Bill and Pym Ball. Bill is an eminent Palaeontologist who was given an 'Oscar' for some of his work in America. Once, after I had been to Charmouth in Dorset, I brought my treasures back to show him: he was singularly underwhelmed. But when I took my fossils from Eigg to show him he actually came down from the ladder where he had been painting, and asked me to get him a map reference for the Natural History Museum in Kensington, where he worked. The crofters' side of the island had been under water; it was a raised beach.

Bill and I felt very ashamed one year; a charming geology student called William was staying at Laig Farm and fossil hunting. He would bring exciting things home every evening. We expressed interest. William gave us a map and precise instructions to find the fossil bed. We found the place all right, but we had to admit to him at supper time that we could not recognise the fossils!

Fossilised oyster shells.

My favourite flowers on Eigg will always be the orchids – there are so many of so many different species. There is no Machair on Eigg as there is on Uist but I am sure there are more orchids on Eigg.

We did once go in September and saw the lovely Grass of Parnassus.

There are two fly-catching plants on Eigg. The Butterwort is attractive, the other kind is *not*, but even less so with a fly in its grasp. I took a slide of a fly caught in the plant and threw it away – it was horrible.

Greater Butterfly Orchid.

Northern Marsh Orchid.

19

LATER, AS TIME HAS PASSED

A S OUR CHILDREN GREW, Ian was the first to go back to Eigg independently. He and one of his friends from Oundle, both aged 16, camped on Laig Farm. They had a great time except when one of the Kirk's cows ate their Edam cheese! Both girls took boyfriends. If the chaps did not appreciate Eigg, they were rejected. It was a case of values and priorities, I think. However, the best return of all was Rosie and Rick for their wedding.

Ian and Rosie took Sophie when she was very small. Ian was sad because he took her to the wonderful half-mile of silver sand at Laig Bay and she did not like sand! However, she did appreciate it once she was a little older, and William loved it. They both walked miles. By the time they arrived on Eigg, Sue and Alastair were running a

Lageorna. Original line drawing by Ronald Brett, 1985.

superb guest house and they stayed there. Peggy Kirk had left Laig and moved into one of the new Council Houses – she had developed very high blood pressure and running Laig was too much for her. Luckily by then D. J. (Peggy's youngest son) and his English wife Kay had come back to live on Eigg and took over the running of Laig Farm as a guest house. So Peggy Kirk's three children now run the three guest houses – Marie in Kildonnan with her husband Colin; D. J. and Kay in Laig and Alastair and his wife in Lageorna.

After two knee replacements I can no longer manage the dreadful mile-long road to Laig Farm. It is a shame, as I would love to go back there. What I like to do is to stay on one side of Eigg at Kildonnan for half the time, then go over to Cleadale on the other side for the rest – a perfect two-centre holiday!

Sue Kirk now runs the new shop so does not have time to cater for guests. However, she still lets Lageorna for self-catering.

20

THE NEW COUNCIL HOUSES

F OR SOME REASON none of the owners would give permission for
Council houses to be built. As soon as the island became the
property of the Isle of Eigg Heritage Trust, building started on some.
They were built in Cleadale and I think they blend very well with
their surroundings.

Tigh-a-Bhlar was up-graded and a second new house added. They
were at the top of the track down to the Catholic Church. "Scruff"
– I don't know his real name – lived in the Tigh-a-Bhlar house. He
is a young fisherman who has come to live on Eigg. Once Peggy

The new Council Houses. Peggy Kirk's and 'Scruff''s houses in the front; the Day Centre,
Dolly Ferguson's and Mary Campbell's houses at the back, the other side of the road.

Dolly Ferguson in her new Council House.

Kirk had made the painful decision to leave Laig Farm after so many years, she moved into the new house next to Scruff. He has been very kind to Peggy and brings her fish that she loves, and cuts the grass for both houses. I love Peggy's new house, named "Mingulay": it has a good-sized kitchen and sitting room, two bedrooms and a bathroom. Unfortunately one window looks over to Laig. It took a long time for Peggy to adjust, but she has settled now. The bonus is that it is right by the main road so people pop in to see her who could not face the mile-long road to Laig.

Behind those two houses, the other side of the road, are two more Council houses. One holds the Day Centre, where the pensioners' lunch is provided, and is used for other facilities. Attached to that is Dolly Ferguson's new house. Dolly used to live in Tigh-a-Bhlar. Once the premises became unfit for human habitation Dolly could not get up the stairs in Tigh-a-Bhlar, so she had to sleep in a chair

The new Tea Room, Shop and Craft Shop, dwarfing the old Tea Room.

downstairs. The Council house is more suitable for her. Dolly is not so well now, so a chain of helpers visit every day to care for her.

A little below those houses is the third pair. Ann Campbell, an artist, lives in one and 'Bobby' Bear in the other.

The wonderful benefit these houses share only with the new building on the pier is that they have a generator in a little hut that gives enough electricity for light all day and for washing machines, etc., twice a day.

It was difficult to believe that in July 2000 it would be three years since the Islanders bought Eigg. So much had happened. The wonderful three-in-one building on the pier was the first success. The next was the conversion of the ruin of a stone-built barn into a delightful house. Every bedroom has a wash hand basin; there is a delightful sitting room and excellent food. It is called The Glebe Barn and is the Field Study Centre and Independent Hostel. They run courses from May until 2nd September on varied subjects, such as: Eigg, the Natural Environment and Landscape History; two painting weeks; courses on Traditional Willow Basketwork and Soil and Soul; an Introduction to the Fauna of Eigg, and Geology and Landscape in the Inner Hebrides. Details of courses can be had from Simon and Karen Helliwell, tel/fax 01687 482417.

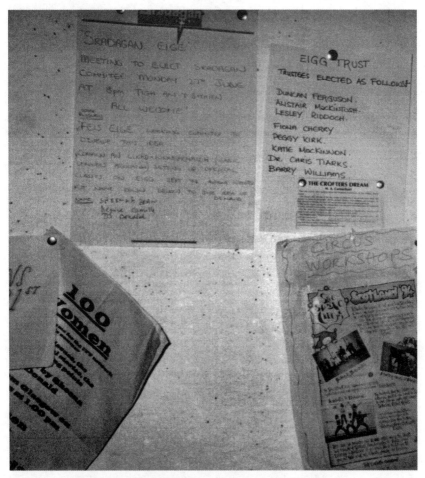

Part of the islanders' campaign to purchase Eigg.

21

So What of the Future?

THE ISLANDERS had been so sensible and not rushed into doing things. They appointed a project manager and another doing feasibility studies. A Gaelic-speaking lawyer came from Lewis and spent a whole week on Eigg sorting out their leases, which they all now own.

However, after so many years of living under one owner of Eigg who had control over so much of their lives, it is heady stuff to find themselves (along with The Highland Council and The Scottish Wildlife Trust) responsible for their own future with no one but themselves to blame should anything not work out. As well as the feasibility study, they are taking great care to discover what prospective buyers of the few surplus houses have in mind for the use of those houses – no more houses standing empty half the year!

Some of the islanders made some lovely crafts to sell in the shop, but had to stop while all their time and effort went on the battle to buy the island. I do hope that they will start again once they get their breath back. So far they have worked brilliantly together – this is essential in a small community.

The Glebe has been a great success, with a different course each week. I hope to attend one in the spring of 2001.

The plans to put a causeway between Eigg Pier and Castle Island seem to be going ahead. Once this is done the harbour can be dredged to make it deep enough for Caledonian MacBrayne's boats to come in to the Pier. The *Sheerwater* only runs in the season and often bad weather prevents the MacBrayne's boats from standing off the island to transfer post, deliveries and people onto the Eigg ferry.

There are only 64 people on the island, with probably less than one-third of those willing and capable of management. Those few people share the various duties (for example, Colin Carr, the former Special Constable, is now the Coastguard). They must be treated as if they were gold, and none of the minor irritations that can occur

The third generation –
William Orr.

in any group should be allowed to cause the loss of even one of them.

They are wonderful, very special people, all of them, and I wish them well for their future with all my heart. It is always terrible leaving Eigg. All our friends gather on the pier to wave. I always leave a bit of my heart behind and wave back until Eigg becomes once again just a distinctive outline on the horizon, with Rhum peaks beind it and the distant Cuillins of Skye – and Ronnie pointing out another whale ...

ISLE OF EIGG HERITAGE TRUST

URRAS ÒUALCHAIS EILEAN EIGE

The Isle of Eigg Heritage Trust
is a partnership between
The Eigg Residents, The Highland Council and
The Scottish Wildlife Trust

http://ourworld.compuserve.com/homepages/eiggtrust
e-mail: 106162,2712@compuserve.com (Maggie Fyffe)
or
JMcDonell@compuserve.com (Jacqueline McDonell)

INDEX